SELF-DEFENCE

This book is written primarily for those who have little or no knowledge of judo but who, nevertheless, would like to be able to defend themselves in the event of a physical attack. It describes easy-to-learn tricks of self-defence used against actual attacks which have taken place, and which have been reported in court and newspapers. First, the attack is discussed, then methods by which the assault could have been averted, and the assailant held, are shown. The latter part of the book includes a few methods for the reader who has studied some, even if only a little, judo.

This book explains and teaches the grips and throws that are useful in this art. It is intended mainly for those with little or no knowledge of judo but who, nevertheless, may find themselves in a position of needing protection against physical attack. The tricks explained are easy to learn yet very effective. This book is also an interesting introduction to Judo, certain principles of which are applied in the teaching of self-defence.

Higher Education Journal

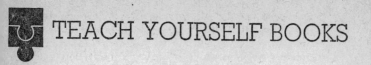
TEACH YOURSELF BOOKS

SELF-DEFENCE

Eric Dominy

Black Belt Holder and British International

Illustrated by

Peter Johnson

ST. PAUL S HOUSE WARWICK LANE LONDON EC4P 4AH

First printed   *1957*
Tenth impression   *1975*

ISBN 0 340 05713 0

Printed in Great Britain for
The English Universities Press Ltd., London, by
Hazell Watson & Viney Ltd, Aylesbury, Bucks

INTRODUCTION TO SELF-DEFENCE

The need for Self-Defence

You have only to pick up a newspaper to read of attacks made, not only on lonely commons, but also in built-up areas to understand the need for a knowledge of self-defence. Even worse, some of these assaults are made on members of the Police force, who at last are receiving instruction on judo from qualified teachers. What makes these attacks such interesting reading is that most of them could have been made harmless by even an elementary knowledge of judo or self-defence. Were a few of these thugs to be collected by the police in a battered condition I'm sure these activities would soon cease.

Most people know and believe that judo is the answer, but think that it is a form of magic for a favoured few, and that years of training are necessary. If a high standard of judo proficiency is to be attained certainly much training is necessary, but this is not required to make self-defence effective. A few weeks under a qualified instructor, that is, one who holds a high judo grade, can produce amazing results. If you are not sure about the qualifications of your local instructor, contact the London Judo Society, 32, St. Oswalds Place, London, S.E.11, and they will advise you.

I have personal knowledge of several incidents in which knowledge of self-defence saved the situation; let me tell you about some of them.

One of our junior members aged 14 had to return home from London Judo Society across the desolate site of some houses destroyed by bombing. One night he was attacked by three youths. He threw one and the second attacked him with a brick—he checked the blow, countered with an arm lock, and threw his opponent who dislocated his shoulder. The third ran away. Our junior was unharmed and not even his clothing was damaged.

Fred Ingram with whom I have often demonstrated self-defence was mobbed by five Teddy-boys. He also tackled them without hesitation and threw three of them; the rest then fled leaving one casualty on the ground. Fred, unfortunately, loathes hurting anyone and it was not until he suffered a broken nose from a butt from a head that he really pitched into his attackers.

Even the ladies find judo effective. Mrs Peggy Merton, my partner in many self-defence displays, was given trouble by four of the Teddy-boy types whilst crossing a car park. She threw the first one to touch her into a pool of mud with a Shoulder Throw, and the rest immediately fled.

The last story is the best illustration of effective self-defence by a person with practically no judo knowledge. A police officer of the Malaya force was on leave in England for a few weeks, and took a few private lessons from George Chew, one of Britain's leading teachers. Soon after he returned to duty he was attacked by a native who tried to strike him down with a lump of stone from behind. Fortunately he heard his attacker, checked the blow aimed at his head, threw his opponent hard and held him easily until more police, called by his wife, arrived.

Well there you are! We certainly do not claim self-defence lessons can make you invulnerable but they obviously offer you a much better chance if you are attacked.

About this Book

'Teach Yourself Self-Defence' is intended mainly for those who have little or no knowledge of judo. More experienced judo people will, I hope, find Part 2, which was written for them, useful and instructive. I will not, however, in the early stages describe the many graceful and effective methods and tricks which depend on basic judo technique. If you have this knowledge already, so much the better. This book describes easy-to-learn tricks of self-defence used against actual attacks which have taken place, and which have been reported in Courts and newspapers. I will describe the attack, then show methods by which the assault could have been averted, and the assailant defeated. Later in the book I will include some methods for those who have studied some, even if only a little, judo.

I am afraid a few judo purists will shudder at a book which avoids the necessity of a lengthy basic training in judo and which describes attacks that are violent and possibly crude. Be that as it may—I am certain of one thing—they are effective.

In many cases I will describe several methods of defence and counter-attack against a certain form of assault. Don't worry about this, try the lot and select that which best suits you or combine one or two. It really does not matter as long as it works. If you practise with a partner, instead of on a dummy, please be careful, these tricks are selected for their effectiveness, not for their grace and beauty.

Judo technique would, of course, help you and if you wish to learn more of the real service of this wonderful sport, I suggest you read the book "Judo" in the same Teach Yourself Series.

CONTENTS

PART I

ix

PART ONE

CHAPTER I

THE BASIS OF SELF-DEFENCE

There is only one basic principle of self-defence. You must apply the most effective weapon as soon as possible to the most vulnerable point of your enemy. At the back of this book you will find diagrams showing the most effective weapons given to you by nature and the most vulnerable points of the body.

Although I say there is only one basic principle, it is better to break it into sections and look at it more thoroughly, especially as I intend to refer back to this continually. The points to consider are:—

1. What is the most effective weapon.

2. Speed.

3. The point to attack—or counter-attack.

The Weapon

Given a choice I would always choose the leg. It is longer than the arm and can deal a heavier blow, and it is much more powerful. So should someone approach you, your kick would make contact before his punch, if both commence at the same time. Therefore the leg is your most effective weapon.

Speed

There is no time to consider the type of defence or weapon to use. Obviously if your kick does not commence until long after your opponent commences his punch the punch will land first, and your defence is useless. Only training can produce results. If you do not consider a few hours training worthwhile, and think the chance of assault is small, you are one of these people who encourage thugs to attack, and no one can help you should an emergency arise.

The point of Counter-attack

Amongst the most vulnerable points for your counter if attacked by a man are the groin, abdomen and knee and if your counter is a kick these are the obvious targets. You cannot however adopt this form of defence against a hold from behind you or at close quarters, so a different form of counter has to be attempted. Here practice and knowledge come to your aid and this is where this book will help you.

Note.

The attacker is shown wearing the black judo jacket in all the illustrations.

CHAPTER II

DEFENCE AGAINST ATTACK, FROM THE FRONT AND REAR

Attacks of this nature can be divided into nine main groups and taken separately.

1. Overhead blows with a stick, knife, stone and so on.

2. Straight and sideways blows aimed at the head, chest or stomach.

3. Downward blows aimed at the stomach or groin.

4. Grips on the hair, clothing and body.

5. Kicks or blows with a knee to the groin or stomach.

6. Butts with the head.

7. Strangles.

8. Grips from behind.

9. How to settle the attacker when he has been forced or thrown to the ground.

Group One

OVERHEAD BLOWS WITH A STICK, FIST, ETC.

Left Hand Defence

You must always move in to meet this form of attack and also turn your body sideways as you do so

Fig. 1

to protect yourself from his knee. The illustration (Fig. 1) shows the attacker aiming a blow at the defender's head with his right arm. Immediately step in with your left foot and turn your body with the left side facing the attacker. This has the double effect of protecting yourself from a kick which I have already mentioned and also bringing you close to your opponent so that you are able to check the blow with your forearm against his arm, and thus avoid a blow on your arm from his stick. If you chop upwards with the bony side of your left forearm leading, that is the small finger side of your arm, your blow against his arm will most probably paralyse his forearm, and make him drop his weapon. In any case strike up and slightly outwards with your arm as there is always the chance that his wrist will bend and even though you check him, the weapon, especially if it is a long stick will continue to deliver a painful blow if directed to the back or side of your head. If, however, you curve your body well forward and chop outwards this cannot happen.

Immediately you have made contact bring your right arm up behind your opponent's attacking arm and *grip your own left wrist*, continuing your movement past him as you do so by advancing on your right foot past his right side. If you keep your body curved well forward you will find he will be bent backward and held in an arm lock. Retain this lock and hurl him backwards to the ground with it. He should hit hard, his right arm being severely wrenched as well. Here a foot or heel placed judiciously in his solar plexus will make a second attack most improbable.

Right Hand Defence

Many people feel more comfortable if they defend with their right arm and if this is so in your case you should parry the right-hand attack with the same upward chop but this time with your *right* forearm, stepping forward with your right foot, as you

Fig. 2   Fig. 3

do so turning the right side towards your opponent (Fig. 2). As you make contact, step forward with your left foot moving behind your opponent past his right side and gripping him round the neck with your left arm, pulling him backwards with it (Fig. 3). If you are fairly strong you can grip your opponent's right wrist with your right hand and lock his shoulder and arm, thus compelling submission (Fig. 3) or alternatively you can clasp your left hand with your right and force him backwards in a very powerful stranglehold. In this hold it is essential to help him off balance backwards. The latter method is in my opinion far better for the lighter person as not so much strength is required. A knee driven into the attacker's back will disable him.

Counter and Throw

Go back to the basic counter (page 18), checking the

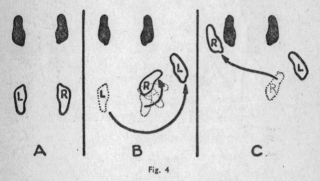

Fig. 4

blow with your left forearm (Fig. 1). This time bring up your right arm and instead of clasping your own left wrist grab your opponent's right wrist, or far better, his sleeve. As he continues to attempt his downward thrust turn to your left pivoting on your right foot and stepping back and to your left with your left foot passing your left foot behind your right (Fig. 4). Turn to your

Fig. 5

left as you do so, bring-
ing your body out of the
direct line of his attack.
Now pull him forward,
sliding your right foot
back against the outside
of his right (Fig. 5) and
pull him forward with
your arms. He should
be thrown across your
outstretched right leg to
the ground.

Defence with a kick

Many self-defence 'experts', that is to say Black Belt
Judo men with an interest in the self-defence side of
Judo, regard the foot as the finest weapon. It fulfils all
the requirements I called for in Chapter 1, and is the
most difficult form of counter-attack to avoid.

Because of the importance of this form of defence I
feel justified in repeating my earlier comments. The leg
being longer and stronger than the arm, even the
lighter and smaller person has a really good chance
of coming off best if this form of defence is
adopted.

In this case your attacker approaches you probably
armed with a stick and you have time to see him coming.
As he may be able to overwhelm you with his strength
it is fatal to allow him to come to close quarters

so you must keep him at a distance with your leg.

As your opponent attacks turn on the ball of your left foot, bending your knee as you do so, and drive your right heel back at your opponent's knee. As you turn, don't forget to keep your eyes on your attacker. Make contact with his knee with your heel as hard as you possibly can, and especially if you are a woman wearing a high fairly pointed heel, it is most unlikely that the attack will be followed up. Should it be, repeat the dose: or again should your opponent double up, as is most likely, as a result of your kick to his knee, attack in the same way again, this time kicking to his groin, stomach or ribs as convenient. It is fatal to kick upward with the toe while facing your opponent, as this form of kick is easy to avoid and even more easily countered—see Chapter 5. The straight driving heel is, however, extremely difficult to stop and almost impossible to counter.

Should you be unfortunate and pushed or knocked on to your back your position is not weakened. This time bring your legs back into a defensive position (Fig. 38) and again strike at your attacker's knee as he comes in, using your heel to strike his knee. Only use one leg to thrust, keeping the other back as an emergency measure (Fig. 38). If your opponent tries to move round to avoid your leg, revolve on your back to keep your legs facing him.

Points to Avoid

1. When standing do not kick higher than is essential, as this makes it more easy to lose your balance and be toppled over.

2. Never kick up at your opponent with your toe as this is easily avoided and leaves you in a very precarious position.

3. If on the ground, only thrust with one leg, keeping the other as a reserve defence.

4. Always keep facing your opponent except when you turn to thrust with your leg when standing. Even here you must keep your eyes on him by turning your head.

CHAPTER III

Group Two

STRAIGHT AND SIDEWAYS BLOWS AIMED AT THE HEAD AND CHEST

Shoulder Drop Counter to a Straight Right-Hand Punch to the Jaw

This counter is really pure judo although in this description I propose to make it as simple as possible and avoid technicalities. As usual the main object is to avoid the attack and the counter is a secondary, although very important consideration. Step in with your left foot and chop upwards with your left forearm deflecting the blow past you with the sharp little finger edge of your arm. Immediately turn to your left on your right foot following the direction of the attacker's blow and grasp his right sleeve with both hands near the shoulder pulling it in the same direction as the blow, that is round to your left. As you do so, continue to turn to your left on your right foot (see Fig. 4) and continue your turn until you are facing the same direction as the attacker. As soon as your leg is firmly on the ground stetch your right leg outside his, making contact with his leg with the part of your own leg just above your ankle (Fig. 5) and pull him over it to the ground.

Variation

Deflect his blow as I have already described, and having done so begin your turn to your left, perhaps  gripping his right sleeve with your left hand. Now as you turn bend your right arm at the elbow and bring the elbow up hard against his jaw. If this is not sufficient you can continue with the throw. Alternatively, as you turn you can bring your knee hard up into your attacker's groin (Fig. 6) and then continue, if necessary, with the throw.

Fig. 6

Counter to a blow aimed sideways at the head

As this form of attack is usually made with some form of weapon such as a stick, the first principle must be as always, to minimise the effect of the attack or better still to avoid it completely. Of course if the attacker approaches from a distance and you have warning, the answer is the kick described on page 22, but I am assuming that the attack is made unexpectedly from close range. Immediately step in with your left foot towards your opponent's right shoulder, stopping the blow by bringing up your left forearm to check his arm with a chopping action from the sharp boney edge. The object of stepping in is to bring yourself inside the arc described by his weapon and render it harmless. As you contact his arm with your left arm bring up your

Fig. 7

right arm and grip his right arm at his shoulder. It does not matter how you do this as long as you hold him firmly and close to you. Now you can, of course, put him out of action by bringing your right knee into his stomach or if this cannot be done bring you right leg through between you (Fig. 7) and hook it behind his right knee. If you pull down with your arms and pull back with your leg he will take a heavy fall.

Counter to a blow aimed at the waist, hips or stomach

The same counter applies whether it is a sideways swing with a stick, or a straight punch to the stomach. A straight thrust with a stick is a most unlikely form of attack. Here again the avoidance is a step in with your left foot and chop down with your left forearm at his forearm. Immediately you can do so counter-attack with your right fist or knee or alternatively you can clasp his jacket near his right shoulder with your left hand and reach forward with your right leg (Fig. 7), bringing your right leg behind his right knee in a hooking movement. At the same time grip his clothing near his left shoulder with your right hand—or around the neck if that is easier. As you pull him back towards you with your hooked right leg you push him downwards and backwards with your arms. Do not be afraid to fall with him as you will be on top.

Group Three

DOWNWARD BLOWS AIMED AT THE STOMACH

This is a most uncommon form of blow and certainly would not be delivered by anyone with experience of boxing. It is however, a most powerful blow and would disable anyone if it landed. The counter is made more difficult by its sharp downward angle and as usual the first object is to avoid it. Again check it with an outward chopping action from your left forearm, at the same time advancing your left foot, thus presenting the side of your body to your opponent in case the blow got through. In this case it will land on your hip and cause more damage to the attacker's hand than it will to you. Once this blow has been deflected or checked, grasp his clothing at his right shoulder or right side, and bring your right leg up behind his right. This throw has already been described and illustrated in Figure 7. Alternatively, you can counter with your right knee, fist, or elbow or with the throw as well if you like.

Counter to a Boxing Type of Attack

It is quite safe to say no one is likely to be attacked

Fig. 8

by a trained amateur or professional boxer as anyone who is prepared both to give and receive blows is far too good a type to attack a defenceless person. However a boxing type of attack is one of the most likely forms for aggression to take. Should an attacker square up to you as shown in Figure 8, do not attempt to counter or fight him at his own game. If the reader is a girl or a light person nothing could be more disastrous. In the case of a right-hand attack such as that shown in Figure 9, ward off his right arm with your left and

Fig. 9   Fig. 10

by stepping in close to him with your left leg push your left arm round his body (Fig. 9) and grip his left sleeve with your right hand. Now step round with your right leg, bringing it back and close to your left (Fig. 10) so that the momentum of your opponent's punch makes him lean up against your back. Hold him in this position, pulling him to his front with both your arms and if you now place your left leg outside his left and turn to your right your opponent will be thrown over your outstretched left leg to the ground. You can also throw him over your hip but this is more difficult.

CHAPTER IV

Group Four

GRIPS ON THE HAIR, CLOTHING OR BODY

I shall describe several methods of dealing with these attacks, but the counters are not really so complicated or numerous as they appear—if they were they would be valueless as one cannot learn and master many different methods without hours of practice each week.

In all these grips, very common ones, the principle behind the counter is the same and a certain amount of practice will help you to adopt the required variation to the immediate need without thinking about it.

Counter to a Grip on the Hair with one hand

This form of attack is most likely to be used against women so it is safe to assume the attacker will be a man and far stronger than his intended victim. In these circumstances it is no use describing counters based on pure judo which require far superior skill to overcome greater strength, but better to keep to crude but effective methods which rely on speed and surprise for their success.

The attacker has grabbed his victim's hair with his right hand (Fig. 11). As illustrated, immediately place your right hand on his and hold it there firmly. This has the added advantage of preventing or at least greatly reducing the pull on your hair. Pivot to your right on your left foot or on your right foot if easier

Fig. 11

making a half turn so that you are now facing the same direction as your opponent (Fig. 12). This will bring your opponent's right arm, outstretched, along your left side. Immediately bring your left arm hard down on his elbow, using your elbow if possible (Fig. 12) and follow with a second backward blow with your left elbow to his body. If your opponent is tall you may not be able to bring your arm down on his, and in this case make your attack to the body at once. You should not have any further difficulty.

As an alternative you can place both your hands on the hand with which he is holding your hair and

Fig. 12

turn to your left, countering with the backward kick to the body described on page 22.

Counter to a two-handed grip on the Hair

Here again immediately pin his hands firmly with your own and turn to your right, pivoting on your left foot. As before you will find yourself close to your opponent with your left side by his right. Immediately release your left hand and drive your left elbow into his body aiming for the abdomen or solar plexus. You can also or alternatively drive your heel into his knee or shin. This is amazingly effective if you are a woman wearing a sharp heeled court-shoe. You could also, of course, bring your left elbow down hard on his right elbow. If you pull his arm sharply towards you as you turn, his arm is in just the position for this attack.

Grips on the Hair from the rear

These do not present nearly so great a problem as one would imagine. The only object of such a grip, or a similar one on the clothing, is to pull the victim close so as this is also necessary for the counter, attacker and victim are for a short period in agreement and this eases the situation. Never pull away in such

Fig. 13

a situation unless you are sure you can break away completely, the object must be close contact. Immediately grip your opponent's right wrist, even if he is holding with both hands. Curving your body forward in order to bring your hips lower than his, and also to ensure that you remain on balance (Fig. 13), pull him forward and drive your hips back into his body, taking a series of short steps backwards if necessary. Immediately you make contact—and make contact with your hips as hard as you can, drop your right leg back outside his right and pull him over it to the ground. Alternatively as you make contact you can let go of his arm and drive your elbow into his body, or use your heel hard on his knee or shin. Any of these moves should free you without much difficulty.

Grips on the Clothing

The methods of breaking these holds which are almost always applied at the level of the attacker's own chest or shoulder are basically the same as those for grips on the hair on page 32. In fact as the attacker's hold is lower on your body it is easier to apply downward pressure to his arms and the counter is more simple to apply and more effective.

A grip, right-handed as usual, is made on your clothing at chest level. A right-handed grip would, of course, be on your left side. Immediately grip his sleeve with your right, or both hands, to keep his hand in that position, and turn to your right on your left foot. As you turn keep pulling his right sleeve so that when your turn is completed (Fig. 12) his arm is outstretched along your left side. Immediately drive your left elbow down on his outstretched arm at his elbow and you should have no further trouble. You can also pull his arm up hard into your left armpit and obtain the lock by lowering your body sharply by bending your knees.

Alternative Counter to a Hold on the Clothing

This is a counter for a stronger person and uses a very effective lock—the wrist lock. Again the attacker grips your clothing at about your chest level with his right hand. Immediately clasp your hands together and place them firmly on the back of your opponent's hand as shown in the Fig. 14. Now take a short and

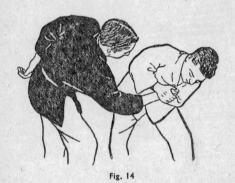

Fig. 14

rapid step back with your left foot in order to extend your opponent's arm and at once curve your body forward and bend your knees, turning to your left (Fig. 14). You must make these movements sharply and you will apply a painful lock to the attacker's wrist. If the movement is made violent the wrist can be broken.

Should the attacker grip with both hands apply the lock to one only, selecting the wrist which is most convenient to you. The effect will be just the same.

Counter to a Grip on the Wrist

Here I must stress again one of the basic theories of judo—always attack your opponent's weakest point with the strongest available weapon. In this counter

Fig. 15

it is essential to apply judo theory, but very little practice with a friend will make this action automatic.

Your opponent grips your right wrist with his right hand. Fighting to free it is useless especially if he is stronger than you, so you must apply your maximum strength against his thumb when he will be completely unable to maintain his grip. To do this immediately dig your right elbow—the elbow of the wrist being

held—into your right side, just above the hip and
apply the pressure against his thumb, driving your
hips forward and upward in a circular movement
thus applying the whole power of your body against
his thumb (Fig. 15). He will be completely unable
to hold you and your thrust will drive his body upright and backwards. Take advantage of this to attack
with your knee or hook your right leg behind his
right knee and drive him backwards to the ground
over it (Fig. 7 on page 27).

ALTERNATIVE METHODS OF COUNTERING GRIPS ON THE
WRIST

Grip on one Wrist

Your opponent has gripped your right wrist with

Fig. 16

his left hand. Step in towards him with your right
foot and using his grip as a pivot turn sharply to
your left, pulling your wrist free (Fig. 16) with a

quick movement as you do so. As in the upward method of freeing yourself you must free your wrist by pulling it out of his grasp between his fingers and thumb.

Breaking a Grip on Both Wrists .

Both your wrists are being held as shown in Fig. 17. Step in with your right foot and swing your arms down sharply, straightening them as you do so (Fig. 18). Continue this movement by swinging the arms

Fig. 17   Fig. 18

outward, twisting them at the same time, so that your hands have the palms backwards (Fig 19). This should bring your body close to that of your opponent but as he will tend to have his body curved forward at this stage, you have freed your wrists (Fig. 19) but cannot make contact with your knee. Instead, as you free

Fig. 19   Fig. 20

your wrists, bend forward and grip your attacker's trousers at the back of his knees and pull sharply towards you and upwards, at the same time butting him hard on the chest with your head (Fig. 20). Your attacker will find himself thrown hard on to his back.

Alternative Method of Breaking a Grip on both Wrists

The counter to this grip is exactly the same as that just described for the hold on one wrist. Both your elbows must be dug into your sides just above the hips, and exactly the same movement of the hip, forwards and upwards, is made against his thumbs. Again he will be forced to release his hold, probably with dislocated thumbs, and you can attack with your knee, or again with the rear throw, or possibly both.

Grip on one Wrist with both hands

This grip will cause more difficulty than the other wrist holds just described, as with a wrist held with both the opponent's hands, the victim if he is to free himself, or herself, must apply a certain amount of strength and

Fig. 21

certainly science. The former is always likely to fail because strength, probably superior strength, is being applied against you downwards, but skill will certainly succeed—although you must apply your own strength as far as possible. Immediately the hold is applied curve your body forward and grip your own left hand, the one that is held, with your right hand bracing your left elbow against your side and driving your hips and left arm up and forward pulling with your right hand in the same direction and a little towards you (Fig. 21), thus greatly increasing the power behind the movement. It is an advantage if you step in with your left foot as you break the grip, as not only does this add to the force but it protects you from a possible kick. In addition it leaves you nearer to him for your follow up attack with your own knee or a throw to his rear. In this hold with both hands it is particularly important to obtain your forward and upward thrust from your hips and to make it in a circular movement, forwards and upwards.

Breaking a Grip on the Arm

This time your right forearm or upper arm is being held by your opponent's left hand. The theory of the counter is exactly the same as that just described for the wrist hold. Move in with your right foot, turn sharply to your left (Fig. 22).

Both these counters must be made suddenly and with as powerful a jerk as possible. If the move is made without warning, not much strength is required and a girl could expect to escape from a man's hold. For this reason it is essential not just to move the arm but to get the whole power of the body, however little, behind it. The more strength you have available the more important it is to use it. This of course applies in all the counters described in this book.

Fig. 22

These moves only serve to free you and if your attacker is stronger than you are, he will no doubt attack you again. It is essential therefore to make a counter-attack. You can do this effectively by changing the direction of your right arm and driving your elbow into his stomach or upward into his face, whichever is more convenient. Alternatively you can disable him by turning and driving your left knee into his groin.

CHAPTER V

Group Five

DEFENCE AGAINST KICKS OR BLOWS WITH THE KNEE

These are nasty and in a fight with the sort of person who might be expected to attack you, are probably the greatest dangers that anyone trained in self-defence will meet. One of the first points raised by people who do not think much of judo, usually because they cannot practise it, is that our technique leaves us open to this form of attack. This is completely incorrect as we always meet an attack with the body turned sideways, even defence and attack in judo as a sport is based on this movement, thus always presenting the solid and more difficult to harm side of the body to your opponent. At least, therefore, we minimize as far as possible the result of such an attack.

If you are attacked in this way you must deal with the situation in this order:

1. Avoid or minimize the attack.

2. Counter attack.

As the kick is a long range weapon and as the knee is used at short range I will deal with them separately.

I think the attack with the knee at close quarters is by far the greater danger.

Avoiding and Countering Kicks

I shall only deal with the unscientific straightforward kick made by an opponent facing you, as this is the only type likely to be met. The judo method described as a form of defence is a most unlikely sort of attack to be made because it is basically defensive.

As your opponent comes towards you, you must always be prepared to meet a kick or knee to the body. Assuming, as usual, the kick is delivered with the right foot, meet the attack by stepping forward and

Fig. 23

to your left, with your left foot and turning your body sideways by withdrawing your right hip (Fig. 23). This has the triple purpose of meeting the attack, and thus making a counter possible, presenting the hip to your opponent instead of the vulnerable parts of the body in case you do not quite avoid the attack and by greatly eliminating the target area, giving you a very great chance of avoiding the kick altogether. As you advance your left foot use your right forearm to chop his leg away from you to your right and having done so continue your arm movement sideways and upwards so that his leg is carried upwards and forwards—that is in the same direction as the kick (Fig. 23). You should find that your opponent is thrown flat on his back and will most likely give his head a well deserved crack on the ground. It is essential to step to your left and sideways in this counter, as unless the sideways movement is made the right-hand counter will be awkward to make. The whole of the right side of his body is also exposed to your counter attack, and, in any case, if you step in you are behind him.

Avoiding and Countering a blow with the Knee

This is not a form of attack which you need fear until you have entered into a close range struggle with your opponent. If you have come actually to grips then, this blow is a serious and likely danger. You cannot avoid the blow completely once it comes but you can either avoid giving him the chance to make the blow or greatly minimize the effects so that it by no means disables you even if it does hurt.

The two basic principles of close combat are to avoid your opponent's knee and not to let him butt you in the face with his head. The latter I'll deal with later, so at the moment we have to concentrate on the former. To do this it is necessary to keep one hip advanced—that is pointing towards and probably in contact with your opponent. If you are right-handed you probably advance with your left hip. The closer you are the less chance he has of using his knee and in any case he can now only develop a very small amount of force and that only against your hip or thigh. In addition you are in a favourable position to use your own right knee or fist, and in addition, providing you are both right-handed you are able to apply your strongest side, your right, against his weakest, his left. Should he attempt to use his left knee you can either withdraw a little further to your right—away from the knee, or check his attack with your right knee or hand. Immediately follow up with a blow with knee or fist to his body as he will now be off balance. Continue by bringing your right leg through between your own body and his to hook his right knee and throw him to his rear.

Group Six

CHECKING BUTTS WITH THE HEAD AIMED AT THE FACE

Here again we have a real danger when in close combat—a danger which can easily be minimized or avoided but cannot readily be countered.

The main danger is to your eyes, nose or mouth from your attacker's head; the greatest menace being produced by the intense pain which results from such a blow delivered to your nose. You cannot counter this sort of blow, you can only avoid giving the opportunity or minimize the effects so that you can still emerge the victor even if such a blow is landed. If you do have to come to grips at close quarters with someone who attacks you then make it really close quarters. If, for example, you step forward with your left leg outside his right, really close to him, he cannot easily attack with his knee and cannot really use his fists whilst

your right leg and arm are free. Similarly if you tuck your head on his right shoulder he cannot use his head on you. If you cannot, or do not wish to get so close keep your head slightly down so that he can only bring his head in contact with your forehead, which will cause no serious damage.

Fig. 24

You have been attacked and have got to close quarters with your opponent. You have warded off, perhaps, a right-hand punch (see page 25) and have stepped in close, placing your left foot outside his right, and your head beside his by his right shoulder (Fig. 24). Attack with your right knee or fist, or both to his body and as he staggers back attack by hooking his right leg behind his knee with your right, and driving him hard over it you will bring off a decisive throw.

Alternatively you can, if it is more convenient, bring your right heel hard down on his right instep. A severe blow here from a woman's high heel will make most thugs discontinue their attack, at least for a moment.

CHAPTER VI

Group Seven

COUNTERS TO ATTEMPTS TO CHOKE OR STRANGLE

The main danger from this form of attack comes from panic rather than the nature of the attack itself. In most cases it is reasonably easy to prevent the attacker obtaining sufficient leverage to be really dangerous, and should he overcome this by forcing you back against a wall or being on top in a ground struggle his very nearness leaves him open to counter attacks with the knee or fingers to his eyes or throat. I have found when teaching judo to the beginner that the slightest pressure on the throat causes immediate panic and frantic efforts to force my hands away, followed by submission. Six months later the same person has learned that the danger is not nearly as great as it appeared, and will coolly check my attack and wait for an opportunity to escape. Should I try the same attack on an experienced Black Belt he would move his head and neck sideways, because he knows that pressure on one side of the throat alone can only cause pain, and then completely ignoring me he would continue with his own forms of attack. The great thing to avoid is frantic tearing at the fingers which some vicious attacker has placed round your throat in an effort to strangle you.

Avoiding and Countering a Strangle Applied standing from the front

The usual form of attack is shown in Fig. 25. The attacker grips your throat with his thumbs on the inside, and attempts pressure against your wind-pipe.

Fig. 25

To obtain an effective pressure he must bend his arms which means that your straight arm can easily make contact even if he has longer arms than you. If you are attacked in this way in the open you have only to back away from the attacker to make his intention impossible. If you move away he cannot secure any leverage. So just walking backwards will make his attack ineffective. To obtain his leverage he must, as I have said before, bend his arms and this brings him closer to you. At this stage a straightforward kick or knee to his body would almost certainly disable your attacker and finish the attack, but if you are bent backwards this may be impossible. Just as effective is to straighten and stiffen your fingers and drive your fingertips hard into his throat. His arms being apart and engaged in his attempts to strangle you make him completely defenceless against this form of counter (Fig. 26). The disadvantage of the kick is that it weakens your own

Fig. 26

balance and should he have turned his hip slightly towards you or your kick miss and strike his hip you will fail in your counter and even worse be pushed over backwards.

Alternatively a sharp turn to your left might easily break his grip and this could be followed by a much more successful kick as described on page 22.

Further forms of defence against this form of attack are described in Section II, which describes the judo version of self-defence.

An Alternative Method

If you are fairly tall or have arms at least as long

as those of your opponent you can use a very effective and painful—to your attacker—method which once more relies on him having to bend his arms in order to obtain sufficient leverage to make his strangle effective. As soon as his intention becomes obvious place the palm of your right hand on his jaw and your left behind his head and jerk his head hard to his left. This can cause severe injury and I certainly do not advise practising it on a friend. The heel of the hand driven under his nose upwards is also very effective.

Counter to a Strangle from the front on the Ground

This is a far more difficult problem to face. I could

Fig. 27

easily describe some spectacular but complicated counters, but to anyone not very experienced in judo they would be impossible to apply. By far the best method of evading such an attack is not to let yourself get into this position.

Your opponent has forced you on to the ground, and is sitting astride you attempting to strangle you into submission or unconsciousness. In order to do this he has to push straight down—that is assuming he has the normal strangle with his thumbs on the middle of the throat, and fingers on the outside (Fig. 27).

Fig. 28

It would greatly ease the pressure if you forced his arms apart and re-directed his effort, but this is not really the answer. You cannot back away to relieve the pressure, nor can you use your knees or fists effectively to his body—you have, as I have already stated, got yourself into a very awkward situation indeed. A strangle of this type does not take long to become fully effective, so the last thing you should do is to attempt to force his fingers away, it just cannot be done, certainly not in time. The best chance for the non-judo person is to make advantage of the full length of your arm and again drive your extended fingertips (Fig. 28) into his throat as hard as possible. Ignore the thought that your attacker will be in agony and making most unpleasant noises, you too will be in this position if you don't counter and counter violently.

Counters to Strangles attempted from Behind

Fig. 29

Here again we meet a form of attack which if applied correctly from a judo point of view is unanswerable, but you are most unlikely to be attacked by an experienced judo man. As, however, an attack from behind is a fairly common occurrence I will describe how this form of attack can be countered most successfully. The attacker will, no doubt, attempt to pull you backwards with his right arm round your neck (Fig. 29). The immediate object must be to recover or retain your balance and to do this you must curve your body forward. Immediately grip your opponent's right sleeve—the arm round your neck and pull it forward. This also has the effect of reducing the pressure on your throat. As you do this drive your hips back into him as hard as you can bending your knees as you do so. This will not only

Fig. 30

enable you to recover but will bring the attacker right off balance. Now push your right leg back outside your opponent's right leg and by turning to your left you'll find that he will be thrown to the ground over your leg (Fig. 30).

Alternatively or in addition you can, when you have pushed your hips back, do some very effective work with your elbows to his body and with your heels to his shins and insteps. These latter blows cause so much pain that you will quite likely be released.

An Alternative Counter to a Strangle from Behind

Even if your attacker has got his hands well round your throat in a powerful grip from behind (Fig. 31), you can escape and turn the tables. Do not panic

Fig. 31

Fig. 32

and attempt to break free by committing the basic mistake of clawing at his hands, but remain calm and take a step to your left with your left foot so that you can bring your right foot through and place it behind his left foot (Fig. 32). Now bend your body forward and grip his trousers at the thighs with both hands. Your right should have been left in front of his body when you moved and as long as you have done this you can grip both his thighs from the outside of his legs as shown in Fig. 33. Now drive your hips to your left in order to utilise the whole of your strength and by pulling his legs for-

Fig. 33

ward from under him and driving your right shoulder to your right against his chest (Fig. 33), you will hurl him backwards to the ground.

How to break a more difficult Strangle from Behind

This time you have been attacked from behind by your opponent who has thrown his right arm round your neck so that his elbow or forearm is across your throat and is pulling you back off balance (Fig. 34). Clasping his hands together grip your opponent's right arm, pulling it forward away from your neck at the same time sinking your body down by

bending your knees (Fig. 35). Now lean forward, straightening your legs as much as you can, in order to completely destroy your opponent's balance and if you have bent forward and got your body low enough you can, by pulling on his right arm, which you are already holding, and by turning to your left throw him hard to the ground at your right side.

Whether or not you can

Fig. 34

straighten your legs to add force as the throw

Fig. 35

depends on your strength and your attacker's weight. If you can do so it greatly adds to the effect of the throw. However, it is quite effective if instead of straightening the legs and thus taking your opponent's weight, you just bend forward enough to bring his balance right forward so that he is balancing his weight on you. Now by keeping him in this position you can make him fall to the ground by just turning to your left and leaning to that direction. As you do this you have to bring the whole of your own weight and balance on to your left leg.

CHAPTER VII

Group Eight

GRIPS ROUND YOUR BODY FROM BEHIND

We can divide these into two types, those which only hold round the body leaving the victim's arms free and those which also pin the arms to the side. In describing means of freeing oneself from these holds I propose to look on the black side, as usual, and assume that the attacker is far stronger than his victim who is quite probably a woman. If this is not the case, of course, the counter is far easier to apply.

Counter to a Grip round the Body from Behind

The attacker's object in taking this hold is to lift you and throw you to the ground, or perhaps drag or pull you down. He approaches from behind and flings his arms round your body at about chest level clasping his hands together to maintain his grip. It is essential to maintain or recover your own balance so your immediate reaction must be to grip your opponent's right sleeve with your hands and pull it forward. This provides you with a form of lever and assists your balance. At the same time drive your hips back into him in a similar manner to that described in the counter to a strangle from the rear on page 59. This not only enables you to recover your own balance but also effectively makes your opponent lose his. By pulling him forward you make him balance on your hips and a quick turn to your left as you pivot to your left on your left foot will turn him off your hip into the ground. In this counter you can again move your right leg back, as shown in Fig. 30 on page 57, against the outside of his right leg and use it as a lever over which you can throw him. You cannot use your elbows on this occasion as your opponent's arms round your body act as a protection for him. You can, however, once more use your heels on his shin, knee and instep.

Counter to a Grip round the Body and Arms

In my opinion this is an easier hold from which to escape than the apparently more simple one just described, mainly because the attacker is much more confident that there is no answer. Your opponent has attacked you from behind, flinging his arms round you and pinning your arms to your sides. This is to the uninitiated a hopeless position in which you can

Fig. 36

only wait to be dragged to the ground. Such need not be the case. You must of course break his grip round your arms and this is done by driving your arms upwards, and outwards with all the power you can muster and bending your knees to lower your body. At the same time curve your body forward driving your hips back into the attacker (Fig. 36). This has the dual effect of breaking his balance forward,

Fig. 37

and thrusting his arms up towards your shoulders, thus releasing your arms. At this stage you should have no difficulty in grabbing his right arm and throwing him to the ground over your right leg which, as usual, you place back against the outside of his right leg (Fig. 37). One point must be emphasised, you must, in the initial movement, thrust your arms up and out-wards as soon and as hard as you possibly can.

How to Defend yourself if Thrown or Knocked to the Ground

Some leading judo instructors are of the opinion that the best defence if attacked is to throw yourself on to the ground and use your legs to keep your opponent at bay. If he persists it is pretty certain that the person on the ground will be able to disable or throw his or her opponent by use of the legs. In many ways I agree that this is so in the case of anyone experienced in judo, but to the uninitiated being on the ground results in a loss of confidence and gives the attacker a decided feeling of superiority which should be avoided. In any case throwing yourself down may be all right on a nice soft clean field in summer, but it loses its attraction when the ground may be a hard muddy pavement in mid-winter. Anyhow, one thing is certain—a good defensive position on the ground is very hard to break and one can counter-attack very effectively from that posture.

You have been pushed, or knocked to the ground by your attacker who, of course, intends to follow up to finish his assault. Immediately curl yourself up, and assuming the attacker to be at your right side, bring your right knee up against your right elbow (Fig. 38). This makes you fairly proof against a kick or push to the body or an attempt to get on top of you. Now by using a convenient hand or leg as a lever as necessary, swivel yourself round so that your legs are towards your opponent and keep that position (Fig. 38). Keep your legs in as shown in the illustration, as in this way they are an effective weapon and a constant threat. Once both legs are outstretched your opponent can work round them and even catch them and push them away, and

Fig. 38

so get in at you. Even if he pushes and you kick him away only kick with one leg, keeping the other as a reserve weapon. Your kicks should be aimed at his knees and you should attempt to strike with your heel. If you keep turning on your back to face him and drive him off with well placed kicks you should be able to spring up and get away, especially if he is crippled from a blow to his knee. Should he manage to catch one foot use the other to drive him off by again kicking to his knee or shin—but this is unlikely as it is practically impossible to catch a blow kept low, and this is another reason for making the knee your target. Withdraw your leg immediately after a kick has been delivered whether or not it succeeds in making contact.

If the attacker is determined, and very fierce after
receiving even a little punishment, he may come too
close to you for his own good and, assuming he
approaches on your right side, you should swivel
to face him and catch his nearest ankle, say his left,
by placing your right foot behind it (Fig. 39). This
stops him stepping back and you should immediately

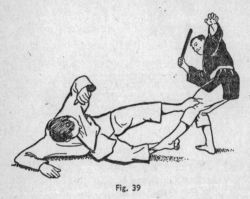

Fig. 39

drive your left heel against his left knee. Not only
will the blow cripple him as before, but he will be
unable to step back to recover his balance and will
be thrown heavily to his back.

Group Nine

HOW TO DEAL WITH YOUR OPPONENT WHEN
HE HAS BEEN THROWN TO THE GROUND

Should you be attacked in a side street or alley there

is no need for further action when you have broken away from your attacker, as it is easy to run to the safety of a more inhabited or better lighted street in the time available before your opponent recovers. Unfortunately the attack might occur when you are walking across a common or equally sparsely populated place and in this case, especially should you be a woman, you will not be able to run to safety before the attacker can get up and have another go. This is even more likely as if he has been thrown by someone not expert in judo or on to turf it is unlikely that he has been put out of action. Well what do we do now? I must make one thing clear at once. I advocate determined and merciless action. A person who attacks defenceless people, and especially women deserves no better and in the interests of your own safety you must take very firm action. This will not only save you but will quite likely result in your opponent refraining from making any other attacks in future in case he receives similar treatment. It also makes it more easy for the police to pick him up later.

You'll find that if you throw the attacker over your right leg in the way I have described already, you will finish up with your right knee near his body. Do not hesitate to drive your knee down into his body if you are in a convenient position to do so. Alternatively you can use your toe to his ribs at the side of his body or a heel to his solar plexus. There are several other forms of attack from this position but they are pretty obvious and depend on the actual position in which you find yourself and your own views on getting your own back. If you decide just to run away make sure that you can reach safety before the attacker can get up and catch you again. Chapter XX shows you the most vulnerable parts of the body and the best methods of attacking them.

Defence against an attempt to snatch your Handbag or Case

In my introduction to this book I said I intended to ignore the usual series of tricks described in so many self-defence books and lessons. This defence is really one of those tricks but this is such a usual form of attack that I have included it although I have made the counter as simple as possible, and avoided the very effective but somewhat complicated method which would come so naturally to the person experienced in judo methods. As a rule a woman holds her handbag loosely—or so I imagine—and anyone coming up silently behind her and snatching it would have little difficulty. The popularity of sling bags however, and the habit of carrying the bag under the arm with the handle held make them harder to pull away easily. The main defence is to hang on to it because bag snatching usually takes place in a crowd.

You are walking down the street, bag or case in your right hand, when our bag snatcher makes his grab with

his right hand—although it does not matter much to the
defence if he grabs with his left hand. Hang on to the
bag if possible, there is no need to do any more than
report to the police if you fail to do this, and curve
your body forward trying to bring the bag round in
front of you. This will make our snatcher tend
to stretch out his arm to follow it and lean forward,
stepping forward with his right leg to your right side.
Now, letting go the bag if necessary, bend forward
and turn your body to your right, catching the legs of
his trousers at his knees with your hands, left hand
on left leg and right hand on right leg (Fig. 40),

Fig. 40

and straighten up your body. Your hands pull his
legs up and forward, and your right shoulder and

elbow drive his body upwards and back (Fig. 41), with the result that he is thrown hard on his back. If your movement is made swiftly and hard it is pretty certain to succeed.

Fig. 41

Although I intend to emphasise this later don't forget that a heavily laden bag is a very useful weapon and swung up hard at arm's length into the face will discourage most attackers.

CHAPTER VIII

THE USE OF EVERYDAY ARTICLES AS WEAPONS

This is a matter of common sense. It is obvious that the pointed and metalled end of an umbrella is a useful and vicious weapon but this has got to be obvious to a somewhat panic-stricken mind in an emergency. There is no need to spend long periods practising swordsmanlike movements on a dummy or before a mirror, what is required is for the mind to get used to the idea—not for the body to practice.

The umbrella and the walking-stick, the latter now more or less obsolete, are ideal weapons. The old-fashioned sword-stick is very little more dangerous than the umbrella ferrule. Always use the point but don't stick out at arm's length like a foil, as it can be easily dashed aside and once your opponent gets inside your weapon it is useless. That is the basis of my teaching throughout this book—the weakness or uselessness of a weapon once one has got past its striking point. Shorten your grip on the stick and use both hands on it (Fig. 42), a two-handed grip halfway down. A thrust delivered straightforward with all the weight of your body behind it is almost unstoppable. Aim for the stomach, just below his ribs and strike upwards. If you strike too high you will hit his ribs, and although this is no doubt extremely painful, it will not disable. The blow to the

Fig. 42

stomach is not only terribly painful but can leave the attacker on the ground, completely unable to breathe. If your attacker is turned sideways to you aim just above his hip—between his hip and lower ribs. The effect will not be quite so devastating and spectacular but you will have no further trouble.

As I said on page 71 the handbag is a useful weapon, especially when you consider the weight of the bag most women carry. The man's brief or attaché case, even if it only contains his lunch is similarly useful. Here the face is the obvious target. Again strike upward. Not only is this very much harder to prevent than a downward blow, but whereas a downward blow will only daze and not disable the attacker the upward blow to the face will again cause extreme pain. A straightforward blow is almost as effective.

I'm told that hat-pins are out of fashion, and most certainly are not worn with coloured scarves, but their usefulness is obvious. Again the ideal target is the stomach or face. In any case I should imagine the threat would be quite enough to prevent an attack.

You will be surprised what a good weapon is provided by a newspaper rolled up and used like a knife straight at the attacker's face. Even if it does not disable, it is painful and very discouraging. Aimed like a sword at the face or throat it can cause quite severe cuts and a great amount of pain.

Forms of Attack not so likely to be met

Glance at the papers and you will find accounts of attacks with knuckle-dusters, razors, bicycle chains and so on. To think of these weapons is frightening, but you must remember that fear is no defence and to the sort of person likely to use these weapons it is an incitement to even further brutality. Fear is no disgrace but it must not be allowed to lead to helplessness. The frightened person is hurt just as much as the hero if he takes the same blow and in fact, if one is afraid to the extent of helplessness the blow is far more certain to land. As long as you react intelligently to any form of attack—and that is all I am trying to help you to do in this book— you stand a pretty good chance of coming out more or less unharmed. Certainly it is probable that your attacker will be hurt far more than you are, which is not only a great consolation but will soon put an end to attacks on people who are presumed to be defenceless.

I think the types of weapon which cause most fear are those used by the sort of youths who tend to go about in gangs—the razor, knife, knuckle-duster and bicycle chain. Most people will immediately say they are most unlikely to meet this type of attack, and I quite agree. There is, however, always a chance that you may get involved in the type of gang warfare which these people wage even at respectable dances and railway stations. There is only one difference, I admit a big one, between this form of attack and those already described, that is if the weapon does make contact it will cause far more damage. There is, however, just as good a chance of avoiding a blow with a weapon as a blow with a fist and once you are inside the weapon, that is past the point at which it exerts its maximum force, the weapon is a liability to its owner.

Let us consider these weapons one at a time, and examine the most effective forms of defence.

The Razor

This is a weapon the mere thought of which causes considerable fright. This fright is the greatest danger because fear produces a stiffness of mind and body which must result in either silly or slow movements or no movement at all. It is only a short weapon so the defence used against it can be the kick described on page 22. If a slash is made at you at arm's length unless you kick you'll have to check the attacker's arm with your forearm in the manner shown on page 18. This is of course an effective counter, but there is a fair chance of your receiving a cut on your forearm. As this is sure to be on the boney outside of the forearm, the little finger side, it cannot possibly be very severe, and must be ignored as you close in to counter-attack with knee (page 26), or rear throw (page 27). I understand from people experienced in the ways of these thugs however, that a slash with a razor is nearly always made at very close range so that your kick would be effective just as would be a blow to his body with your knee.

Fig. 43

Alternatively attempt to knock the attacker's right arm—his attacking arm—outwards to his right with your left forearm at close range (see Fig. 1 on page 18), stepping in with your left foot as you do so. Immediately you have contacted his right arm with your left, pivot on your left foot to your left, and using all the weight of your body as you turn, crash your right elbow to his jaw (Fig. 43). If necessary you can continue with your knee or a throw. As an alternative you can use the throw to his rear by hooking his right leg with your own right leg.

The Bicycle Chain

This is a very unpleasant form of attack which is almost impossible to avoid completely. It causes very considerable pain and superficial injury, but if you can take the force off the blow, it will not disable to the extent that the fight cannot be carried back to the attacker. Two points about it make defence a far more happy proposition than it appears at first thought. First it is a weapon which as a rule is used only in fights between gangs of toughs and is very seldom used against the public. Secondly as an effective weapon it can only be used once as it requires far too long a time to bring it back for a second attack. At any rate the attacker should only be given opportunity for one such attack.

Should you be unfortunate and meet this form of attack you will be greatly helped if you are carrying a walking stick, umbrella, shopping bag, case, or anything which can be used to stop the chain. A

stick held up to catch the chain about half-way down
its length will stop the blow completely, as the chain
will wind itself harmlessly round the stick and a
quick twist will not only disarm the attacker, but
leave you with your stick which should be used

Fig. 44

like a bayonet (see page 73). Even a rolled up newspaper or magazine can have this effect. Anything
else available like a basket will also check the blow
and make the chain wind up. Should you be empty
handed you'll have to chance being hit while you
counter-attack because after all, you'll certainly be hit
if you do nothing. Step in and try and check his arm
just above his wrist (assume his right) with your
left forearm, as low down your forearm as possible.

That is near your own wrist. Check his arm outward to your left, but in particular upward, so that the chain carries on its movement from your left to right above your head (Fig. 44). Now the weapon is past you and useless, you can move in as usual with your right leg or knee. It is particularly important to step in close to him as you check the attack as, if your check fails, at least the chain will only catch you across the back. As you check his arm duck your own head behind your own left shoulder.

The Knuckle-Duster

Here is a form of attack which must be dealt with in exactly the same way as the counter to the bare fist punches already described. The only difference is that it is far more vital that you avoid the initial blow. Unless you meet an experienced and heavy punching boxer, and this sort of chap like a good judo-man will never misuse his skill, you will seldom be disabled by a single blow, and often a judo-man will take one or two blows to the body in order to make contact and use his skill most effectively. An opponent wearing a knuckle-duster is, however, a far different proposition. A blow from a metal-clad fist can mean a broken jaw, or severe cuts and bruises and certainly you will not be able to take any further defensive action. It is essential that your defence is effective and that your first counter-attack is sufficiently severe and accurate to ensure that no second attack is made against you.

Methods of Practice

I do not advocate constant practice, partly because it is not necessary, but mainly because I feel certain that the average reader will not do it and anyway if it is really necessary I have completely failed in my object in writing this book. I am certain that the reader who tries these moves a few dozen times each until he or she is thoroughly familiar with the general idea will be just as likely to emerge unharmed from an attack, as the person who works an hour a day on the moves I have described. In fact I feel he will have an even better chance because where the hour a day person tends to get set in fixed methods of dealing with certain attacks and will fail if something outside his knowledge occurs, the person with only a general idea is far more likely to adapt his much more limited knowledge to the situation.

What then do I advocate? Well most people would feel much better in themselves if they were a little fitter. Readers who play tennis and other games would play better and enjoy their games more, if they were fitter and their bodies more supple. Well then, why not spend about 15 minutes a day, preferably on rising, using my counter movements as exercises? Exaggerate all the movements, turning your body by moving your hip first, this is a really fine abdominal exercise. Make your movements with the knee and hip relaxed. Try and move your arms with the shoulders relaxed instead of tensed and stiff. Relaxation is the secret of fitness and this is a good opportunity for you to practise it.

A great friend of mine has built a very simple dummy in his garden which he uses to practise judo. It could be used just as well for pure self-defence

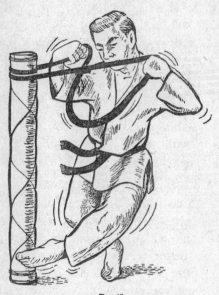

Fig. 45

exercises. If you look at the drawing of this dummy (Fig. 45) you will see that it is quite simple, consisting of no more than a post which has been padded. The two arms are no more than a bicycle inner tube fixed to the "body". Now let us see how you could use the dummy to practise the counter to a blow (page 18).

Imagine the arm of the dummy in a position for a downward blow at your head, just as you would expect your attacker to be with his arm upraised over your head, and having done that, place your-self fairly close at what you consider to be a reason-able distance for this form of attack. Now commence your counter by checking the imaginary downward blow with a cutting blow upward with your left arm and then continue your counter just as described on page 18. You can try out all your counters in this way.

It does help to get friends to co-operate with you when you are trying out the counters and move-ments I have described, because you will find that various people react in different ways to your counters. I find this when I demonstrate self-defence at dis-plays and clubs. Some "attackers" both friendly and otherwise will immediately withdraw when you check their attacks and try again, whilst others will con-tinue with their initial movement attempting to obtain success, through overwhelming strength and persistence. Each method requires different treat-ment, but the counter can always be found in those described, and although you will have to use mental flexibility to adopt the correct method, you should not have much difficulty.

Counters to Hold-ups with Revolvers

As I said at the beginning of this book I do not consider that many of the numerous tricks described in some books on the subject of self-defence have any value. It is therefore with great hesitation that I include the defence against attacks with firearms. These counters have, however, been tested—with blanks—time after time, and I am convinced that it is impossible for the attacker to pull the trigger in time to hit you as you turn out of the line of the bullet. At a recent demonstration using blanks and working with a person who was determined to prove that I could not avoid his shot, I received a burn from the flame from the pistol, but the position of the burn showed conclusively that I would have avoided the bullet even though my opponent had been pulling the trigger almost to firing point, and was waiting for me to move. This then, I feel, justifies my including these forms of defence.

An interesting point which is worth noting is that according to the press a very large proportion of armed hold-ups are made with unloaded or toy revolvers or pistols. The attacker knows that the fear caused by his weapon will almost certainly be sufficient for his purpose. This and the points I have already mentioned, in my opinion, take the defence I will describe, out of the "trick" and into the practical self-defence class.

There is one final point to remember. It is essential that these forms of defence be tried only when the muzzle of the pistol is touching you or is at least very close to your body. Should the attacker with the pistol be some feet away these defences are not effective and I can only leave it to your judgment whether you take any counter action.

Revolver Hold-up from the Front

The attacker holds you up holding his revolver

Fig. 46

against your chest or stomach—you have raised your hands in the approved melodramatic manner. Now, without warning step back with your right foot or forward with your left, turning your body to the right as you do so, and at the same time strike down and to your right with your right arm, as usual using the sharp edge of your right forearm (little finger side) to strike his arm between his wrist and elbow (Fig. 46). Your turn takes your body out of the line of his shot, even if he fires, and the blow of your right arm drives the pistol well away from

Fig. 47

you, and may even force him to drop it altogether. Continue to turn until you are facing the same direc-

Fig. 48

tion as your attacker, and slide your right arm round his right arm from underneath (Fig. 47), holding it against your chest (Fig. 48). Swing your left arm back at shoulder level forcing your opponent back as shown in Fig. 48, and you will find that you are applying a painful arm lock to his right arm. At this stage you should have no further difficulty as a wrench backwards with your right arm and a drive back with your left arm and elbow will disable him completely.

It is also possible to counter by stepping in with your left foot and striking at his pistol arm with your left arm driving it outwards to his right (your left). Now clasp the back of his right shoulder from underneath his armpit, and hooking his right leg with your own, drive him back and down over it. Your arm being under his shoulder should wrench that shoulder severely and make him drop his revolver.

Revolver Hold-up from Behind

Here again the main object must be to get your body out of the line of the bullet before your opponent can pull the trigger. The position is very similar to that in the attack from the front, but in this case the attacker is behind you holding the revolver with the muzzle against the small of your back. Again turn your body to the right by stepping back with your right leg, and as you do so bring your right arm down sharply against the outside of his right forearm. Here you can again continue your turn until you face the same direction as your opponent, and by flinging your left arm back against his chest

Fig. 49

or throat and pulling his right arm sharply across your chest you can disable him (Fig. 48 on page 85).

Fig. 50

An alternative method of dealing with this form of hold-up is to chop downward with your right arm

as already described, thus driving his pistol away from
you as you turn, but this time continue your turn
until you face him, driving his right arm upwards
with your right arm or elbow as you do so (Fig. 49).
This time you make a complete turn on your right
foot and continue to push his arm up until you can

Fig. 51

use your left arm to continue the upwards movement.
Now bring your right arm behind his right and
grip his jacket (Fig. 50) or your own left wrist (Fig.
51). You will find you have applied a painful arm
lock if you keep moving in that direction (Fig. 51).
You can either disarm him in this position or throw
him to the ground with the arm lock and disarm him
in your own time.

This movement sounds complicated but is not nearly so difficult as it appears in practice. I have included it because it is a very good co-ordination exercise, and in addition—it works.

CHAPTER IX

HOW TO FALL IF THROWN

It is possible that the first knowledge you have of an attack on you is being pushed or hurled to the ground. This, anyway, is the impression gained from reading the newspapers. In most cases this is the end of the struggle, if it can be called a struggle, because the victim is usually too winded and shaken or frightened to continue even if no further injury has been received from the fall. For this reason I include a chapter on what we call in judo "break-falls". The pure judo enthusiast no doubt will turn up his nose at this because I have stated that, except in the special section at the end, I am not writing for the judo man, but rather for people without the time or inclination to study the sport. Let me make clear at once, therefore, that I do not intend to explain judo breakfalls in detail, you can read of these in my book "Judo" in the same Teach Yourself Series. My aim is to explain here a shortened and adapted but effective form of fall based on those we teach beginners at judo clubs.

Falling—Basic Principles

There are three main principles which, if they are

observed, will make your falls as painless as possible. Certainly the method of falling I am about to describe will rule out the chance of concussion and other head injuries, and thus enable you to adopt without delay a defensive position on the ground (see page 66), ready to continue the struggle. Well, what are these three principles? They are quite simple and really just common sense.

1. Take the fall with the body relaxed.
2. Keep the body curled up.
3. Avoid falling with your opponent on top of you—Be on top yourself if possible.

These are very simple principles and are pure common sense and what you would expect if you gave a little thought to the matter. Despite this, they cannot be followed unless the victim of the attack keeps his nerve and has done some, even if only a little, practice. A frightened, tense person cannot remain relaxed whilst falling and if you are not relaxed you will not be able to follow my second and third principles.

1 Take the Fall Relaxed

Relaxation is essential to all forms of sport and exercise. If the body is tense whilst falling it is impossible to exercise any control over the fall and all the vulnerable points such as the head, shoulders, knees and so on will be exposed to injury. This happens because there is a very good chance of them striking the ground stiff and rigid on account of your tensed condition, perhaps with the weight of your opponent's body on top of you. If the fall is taken relaxed at least the shock only affects that part which actually strikes the ground, and is not transmitted all over the body. For example if you fall with your body tense with fear and strike the ground with your back, not only is your back damaged, but your head will jerk back and you will be lucky to escape concussion, at least to a minor degree. If, on the other hand, the fall is taken with the body "soft" then the worst that can happen is a temporary disablement caused by the breath being knocked out of your lungs. If you keep your body curled up as you fall even this minor injury need not occur.

2 Keep the Body Curled up when Falling

This is just as vital as our first principle. I have already explained that the main danger to anyone taking a fall is to the extremities, head, arms, shoulders, base of the spine and so on, but this danger can be very greatly reduced. All falls should be taken with the body curled up, thus protecting the extremities at the neck and base of the spine as well as the head, arms and legs. For example imagine a much stronger person attacking you from the rear by placing his arm round your neck and hurling you over backwards. The obvious danger is that you hit the ground with your back and shoulders, your head flies back and hits the ground and you are there unconscious —completely unnecessarily—as a result of the attack.

Now look at the same attack made on a person who knows how to fall. The attacker's arm goes round his victim's neck and because of the complete surprise the victim is hurled over backwards. This time, however, the fall is taken with the body curled up and relaxed so that contact with the ground is made with the body turned slightly towards the side so that the spine does not hit the ground. As the body is curled up you roll so that not only are you unhurt—or at least comparatively unhurt, except perhaps for a few bruises if you are thrown on to a hard surface such as the pavement—but your rolling fall takes you away from your attacker and enables you to get up as part of your rolling movement if you wish to do so. Being curled up your head is kept well clear of the ground.

Falling Backward

Squat down on your heels with your head well tucked in and your arms in front of you (Fig. 52). From here just roll back keeping your head well in all the time and your legs up. It does not matter how far you roll, but if you tend to go right over do so over one shoulder, and not directly over your neck, in order to avoid any strain to the neck or shock to the top of the spine. Your arms kept across and in front of your body are free at your

Fig. 52

sides (Fig. 53). On a soft surface they are used to beat the ground as you fall. At first take it very easy

Fig. 53

and then gradually increase the speed and force of your fall until you can throw yourself backwards from a squatting position into a roll. Take your time reaching this stage and always stop if you feel any jar to the neck, especially any tendency for the head to snap back as you hit the ground; this can cause a severe headache. Don't overdo this as this is not a full breakfall, just a utility version for people not trained in judo.

Falling Sideways

Take up the squatting position shown in Fig. 52

once more, but this time roll sideways and slightly
to the rear, that is to say in the direction of the left
or right shoulder (Fig. 54). Again it does not matter

Fig. 54

how far you roll, the main thing is to keep the body
curled up and the head tucked in rather as if you

Fig. 55

were looking down at the buckle of your belt. Your
left arm is kept across and in front of your body.

When you feel confident about this, become a little more ambitious and stand up. This time bend your left knee—the more you bend this knee the nearer the ground you will be, and the easier the fall and bring your right foot sideways across the front of your left foot. Keep on moving it across and in time you will find that you have to fall. Fig. 55 shows this movement clearly. Again take your time over this until having become completely happy about falling to your right you start again to your left in exactly the same manner.

Falling Forwards

This is unlikely to occur, certainly it can be considered a rare type of fall to have to take, but should you be pushed or knocked down from the rear you would fall in this direction, forward. In addition it is important because it does not follow all the principles of the other falls. The position in which to fall is shown in Fig. 57, but it is far too ambitious to attempt this at first. To start with kneel down and beat the floor with your forearms, striking with the whole of the arm together from elbow to fingertips, so that the forearm strikes the floor absolutely flat. This avoids injuries to fingers, wrists and elbows (Fig. 56). The arms act as shock-absorbers and are placed at shoulder distance apart so that they give and allow the body to come in between the arms slightly in exactly the same way as a car shock-absorber works.

Get quite used to this movement and then try the fall from a slightly greater height, such as a kneeling position, gradually increasing the height until you can throw yourself from a standing position.

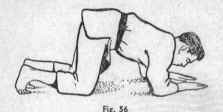

Fig. 56

It is essential to keep your body up as you fall, taking all your weight on your forearms and toes.

Fig. 57

This is done to protect your knees, head and abdomen which otherwise might be injured on contact with the ground (Fig. 57).

Forward Rolling Fall

This is a difficult method of falling to master, but is very useful if you are pushed over forwards or even fall forward when running. From the point of view of self-defence it has the advantage that it requires

co-ordination and relaxation and a certain amount
of courage, and is therefore a really good physical
and mental exercise. This applies also to the other
method of falling forward just described, but to a
lesser extent. Great care must be taken in the early
stages because it is quite easy to injure a shoulder
when practising the fall, but this danger vanishes as
you become more proficient and more confident,
as this enables you to relax.

As usual start learning this fall as near to the ground
as possible, in this case by kneeling down. Kneel on the

Fig. 58

right knee with the right foot and arm forward with
your hand on the ground. Fig. 58 gives you the idea
although this actually shows the more advanced stage of
the fall from the standing position. As usual the object
of this type of breakfall is to take the fall with the
body relaxed to reduce shock and curled up to protect the spine and in addition to protect the head.
In order to do this you commence with the palm or

edge of the right hand, the little finger side, on the floor (Fig. 58) and roll forward so that the contact with the floor continues along the right arm and shoulder across the back and you finish on your left side in exactly the position described. for falling to the side. Fig. 54 shows this position but done on the right side. The roll will not only take you away from your opponent but will also bring you to your feet facing him again if you allow the momentum to carry you on.

This fall is very difficult at first although once mastered you will wonder where the difficulty lay, so I will describe it in detail. First take up the kneeling position I have described with your right foot and arm forward, then roll forward slowly over the right shoulder—not the head as in a gym forward roll. As you roll over the shoulder the slight sideways turn which this gives takes you round on to your curled up back and on to your left side. If your head is well tucked in as it ought to be it will be kept well clear of the ground and neither your head nor neck will receive any jar from the shock of the fall.

Now get more ambitious and stand up again with right foot and arm forward with the palm or little finger edge of the right hand on the floor. Push yourself forward slowly with your left foot and roll along your right arm over the shoulder and back again. Fig. 59 shows the half-way stage in the fall. The right arm is kept straight but relaxed all the time. Straight to keep your head clear of the floor, its collapse would bring your head and shoulders down hard, and re-laxed to prevent injury to the elbow, wrist or shoulder. This is the reason that you turn your right hand inwards on the mat at first. If you think of it you will see that any exceptional strain on the arm will bend it the correct way and not cause any injury to it.

Fig. 59

When you are really happy with this, try throwing yourself and then practis-ing on the other side, left- hand and foot forward.

Note.—I have described a very simplified form of these falls, the judo method of falling is described fully in "Judo" in the "Teach Yourself" Series.

CHAPTER X

BREAKING HOLDS ROUND YOUR NECK

This is a popular schoolboy grip and is generally called the "chancery" hold. From my rather distant memories of school days, I recall that the hold was considered more or less unbreakable and once a victim to it you had your head or body punched until you were forced to cry for mercy. In a real brawl or attack falling into this hold, which is very easy to do, would have a much more serious result and anyone without some knowledge of methods of escape would be fully at the mercy of the attacker. The hold can be applied from either front or rear, each being equally effective or deadly according to your point of view.

Hold round Neck from the Front

In this hold you are facing your opponent, and having got into a crouch, possibly to protect your face from punches, you have got too close to your opponent who has managed to get his right arm round your neck and is pulling your head with pressure on your throat up under his armpit (Fig. 60). Because he is pulling you forward and up you are

unable to punch him with your right fist and your
left is too far away to be brought into action. If you
push him backwards—if you can, which is unlikely—
he will fall on his back with his weight on your head.
If he holds firmly you cannot pull your head out
either backwards or sideways, and, your body being
bent forward, not only are you unable to touch him

Fig. 60

with either feet or knees, but in addition you cannot
bring your right fist, the only one with which you
can hit him, into action with any force again because
of your unfortunate position. What then is the solu-
tion? There are two, neither being particularly easy
but both effective. It is obvious that the only
direction in which you can apply any force is forward,
in fact your bent forward position adds power to
your movement. Just to push forward, however, is

hopeless because he will expect that and move back
as you advance, keeping you both in the same rela-
tive positions. Immediately, therefore, advance your
right shoulder towards your opponent, bringing
it into contact with his body near his hip if possible,
and by pressing against him with your shoulder

Fig. 61

you can reduce much of the pressure on your neck.
Now, by bending your body forward even more
and forcing down with your shoulder you can make
him bend his knees, and at once put your arms round
his knees, as soon as you can reach, clasping your
hands behind his legs if possible, and by pulling
towards you with your arms and driving to your
right front with your right shoulder you will bring
him down heavily on his back or left side, the side
away from your head. Figure 61 shows your position
for this counter-attack. The shock of his fall may

make him let go of your head instinctively to protect himself from the fall, and if he does not do so
it is most likely that he will hit his head hard on
the ground as he falls, sufficiently hard to daze him
even on a soft surface. Then you can escape with
ease.

The alternative counter is similar in principle
but in this case you drive upwards instead of down.
The position is the same as that shown in Fig. 60,
in which your head is held under your attacker's
right arm and you are unable to counter-attack with

Fig. 62

blows. This time drive your body upwards forcing
your head and shoulder up into your opponent's
armpit and to his rear. This will force him to his
toes and in addition bring you close to him as you
have straightened up your body. In fact you are now
close enough to grip his body or clothing with your

hands. Do this and pull him even closer to you and holding him tightly hook your right leg round his right knee. Keep driving your head up and back and at the same time hook his right leg towards you turning to your left as you do so and pushing him back and down with your hands (Fig. 62). He will be thrown heavily to his back. It is essential to turn in order to ensure that your head is not trapped between his body and the ground as he falls and in addition the turn will make him fall with your weight on top of him.

Chancery Hold from the Rear

This is a really wicked hold as your opponent is left free to strike your head and face without reply. You are behind your attacker with your head firmly trapped by his right arm round your neck. This position is shown in Fig. 63. You will see how his left hand is free to punch. Your counter must be quick, because if you take much of this punishment your fighting ability will be gone.

Fig. 63

The attacker gets you into the position shown in

Fig. 63, and at once you push forward and down manoeuvring until you can obtain a grip on his clothing, as high up as possible. As soon as you have this bring your left foot up behind his left leg at knee level and hurl yourself backwards, and to your right, circling on your right foot. Pull him in exactly the

Fig. 64

same circle with your hand (Fig. 64). He will be thrown very heavily over your left foot on to his back.

Chancery Hold from the Rear—an Alternative Counter

As an alternative, having made all your preliminary efforts to break your opponent's balance forward, you will find you can grip the legs of his trousers with your hands directly behind his legs and slightly below his knees. Continue to lift and push forward with your head, neck and shoulder and also lift and push forward with your hands. Your attacker will be run forward at an ever increasing speed until he releases you or is thrown forward on to his face. Even should he release his hold round your neck he probably will still be hurled on to his face, the only difference being that he will now have his hands free to protect his face from contact with the ground. This counter may appear to be amusing when in print and is certainly funny to spectators, but it is devastating and wickedly effective.

CHAPTER XI

DEALING WITH ATTACKS BY TWO
OR MORE OPPONENTS

This is an altogether different problem and requires tactical defence and attack in addition to the basic self-defence movements you have been practising already. In fact the difference is very similar to that in good class lawn tennis in which doubles is a more difficult game than singles to play really well. Not only do you have two opponents to play against, but you have to position yourself with skill as well as watch the ball. In self-defence against two or more attackers you also have to position yourself in relation to your opponents with skill and care.

As I made clear in the early pages of this book no good judo man claims that judo or self-defence skill makes you infallible but it does give you a very much better chance than the unskilled person. If only one weak and puny specimen of a man comes up behind you and hits you over the head with a bottle the judo expert will be just as unconscious as anyone else—but the judo or self-defence expert would be more alert and less likely to fall easy victim

to such an attack. Now this is the position you have
to avoid if you are faced with two or more opponents,
actually facing them is just the right description.
You must keep facing them and not let one get behind
you or out of your sight, certainly not for long enough
for him to attack. This is where your tactics come in.
If you are attacked in an open space keep moving
back, manoeuvring so that you can watch both of
them. Tackle them firmly one at a time by suddenly
moving forward with a rapid kick or blow. When
the chance to throw comes along try and throw one
on to or against another.

You might be faced with two opponents one of
whom gets behind you and grabs you round the
body, whilst the other attacks from the front as you
are being held. Use the first man's hold on you to
help you. It is most unlikely that he will want to
allow himself to fall over backwards, so you can
allow him to take your weight with very little danger
of being pulled over to your rear, because that would
involve his falling underneath you and, in any case,
the person untrained in judo or self-defence usually
fears getting on to the ground. As the second attacker
approaches to strike or rob you allow the man behind you to take all your weight and taking your
feet off the ground for a second, kick at the front
man's knees, groin or stomach (Fig. 65). Immediately he is driven off for a moment or disabled,
put your feet back on the ground without delay,

curve your body forward and throw the man hold-ing you from behind as described on page 63. If he falls hard on his friend all the better.

Fig. 65

The same principles apply if you have to meet an attack by three men. Manoeuvre so that it is as difficult as you can make it for any of them to get behind you and make them get in each other's way as much as possible. If one grabs you from behind despite your efforts try and tackle each of the others in turn with a kick. Quite a possibility is that two will grip of your arms each with the third attacking from the front. Again use the hold on your arms to swing yourself up for a long range and vicious kick and then tackle the men at each side of you. Pull the man on say, your right in towards you, close to your side, then lunge to your right, hooking your right leg round his right knee, and with a violent push to your right with your shoulder drive him over your right leg to the ground (Fig. 66). Alternatively, if this is not possible pull the right-hand man in towards you and this time push out your right leg behind him as far as you can. Then swing

Fig. 66

your right shoulder and arm back violently and he will be driven over your left leg on to his back. Immediately swing round to your left to face the left-hand man and either strike him hard with your knee or fist, or continue your turn and throw him by hooking his right leg with your right and driving him over it to the ground, as described on page 27.

More opponents can be dealt with in this way, particularly if you have a knowledge—even a small one—of judo. Part II of this book will aid you in this respect as it deals with self-defence for people who have studied or will study judo

PART TWO

CHAPTER XII

JUDO FOR SELF-DEFENCE

When the English Universities Press and I origin-
ally discussed the layout and contents of this book
the intention was to confine it to a fairly limited
number of self-defence tricks which would be sufficiently simple to be carried out by anyone who was
prepared to do a little practice but had no knowledge of judo whatsoever. As I worked on the manu-
script I came more and more to the conclusion that
a section was essential which would link up the "crude"
self-defence reader with the "judo as a sport" purist.
I discussed this with leading instructors of London
Judo Society and opinions varied from complete
agreement with me to absolute disapproval. The
position was much the same when I passed the question
to the publishers. Finally the editor left the decision
to me and as a result Part II of this book deals with
comparatively simple judo throws and tricks as
applied to self-defence. I am certain it will be of
interest to the exponent of judo, because it is
based on questions which I am always being asked
when visiting judo clubs, and in addition will be
sufficiently simple to be followed by the reader with

no experience whatsoever of judo. It would perhaps help readers if they read the companion book in the "Teach Yourself" Series, 'Judo', in conjunction with this section or pay a visit to the local judo club, where I am certain visitors will be made welcome. Even better as a basis for self-defence take a judo beginner's course at a good club. This should not be expensive, but it is advisable to ensure that beginners are looked after on a course specially designed for them, preferably under an instructor holding Black Belt grade. I will always be pleased to advise in this subject and strongly suggest readers within reach of London to pay an evening visit to London Judo Society where they will be able to watch some of our leading teachers at work. The Society with its many Black Belts always welcomes visitors but I suggest that the visit is confirmed first by letter or 'phone. The address is, London Judo Society, 32, St. Oswald's Place, Kennington Lane, London, S.E.11. 'Phone: Reliance 5082.

Judo Principles applied to Self-Defence

The basic theory of judo is known to everyone, "give way to strength", but it is generally misunderstood. It does not mean victory by non-resistance, but rather riding the punches as in boxing and then using your opponent's own efforts to throw him. Everyone has seen boxing matches even if only at the pictures, and you must have noticed how often fighters throw a vicious punch and lose their balance staggering forward when it misses its target. If then this "target" instead of moving back or attempting a counter-punch pulled his opponent forward or stuck out his foot for him to trip over, or even both, that opponent would be thrown heavily to the floor, or rather would throw himself there. This is the theory of judo as applied to self-defence—you avoid your attacker's blow and pull him in exactly the same direction as that in which he aimed his punch or attack and at the same time use your foot, or hip, to trip him up. I will try and make this completely clear with some examples and some of Peter Johnson's drawings. In each case the nature of the attack does not matter at present, I'll describe various types of attacks when you have got the theory clear in your mind. You can imagine the attack to be with fist, stick or knife, because the same theory applies to the counter to each.

Consider a push or punch with the right hand against your left shoulder or jaw, a very common form of attack. Imagine an attacker pushing at your shoulder, and you, with no knowledge of judo, resisting by pushing back at him. This becomes a trail of strength with the stronger man winning. Suppose instead you react to his push by moving back in exactly the same direction as he is pushing. His push then will have no effect, and you will not even feel it as long as you continue to retreat. This is in effect resisting by giving way. But to resist an attack is not enough, you must counter to avoid a second and perhaps more violent effort on your opponent's part. So instead of just retreating in the direction of the push you grab the attacker's right sleeve, and pull him in the direction of his push, and if you turn to your left by turning on your right foot you not only give him nothing at which to push, but your pull brings him forward off balance. Continue to turn and pull and he will probably stagger forward advancing his right foot to recover. Now if as you turned you had stuck out your left foot against his right shin instead of lunging forward with his right leg to recover he would have fallen over your outstretched foot and taken a heavy fall.

This is the simple theory of judo. It is simple in theory, but difficult to effect without considerable practice. Let me repeat the theory—just get out of the way of his push, helping him along if possible, and leave him an odd leg, foot, or hip, to fall over.

There is another way of getting out of the direction of his attack, that is to drop down below his centre of gravity, which is at about the level of his hips. Once more the attacker pushes and the defender resists by pushing back at him—force against force and again the stronger man wins. If instead of doing this the defender bends his knees and pulls his attacker forward the result is that the attacker tends to push at nothing and lean over his intended victim. Now the defender should turn his body as he pulls at his opponent's right sleeve, so that he faces the same way, and if he sinks his body by bending his knees so that his centre of gravity is well below his attacker's the position is reached where the attacker's continued push helped by your pull actually causes him to hurl himself over his victim's shoulder or hip to the ground.

This then is the theory on which you have to work if you are using judo—real judo—as a means of self-defence instead of a few of the cruder judo tricks with very little science behind them. Although I shall draw your attention to these principles when describing actual movements, I will not constantly emphasize the basic theory as I did in the "Teach Yourself" book 'Judo'. Rather, as I have said, I am taking it for granted that the reader of this part of the book is a practising judo enthusiast, or has at least practised sufficient judo to know these principles, or intends to learn to practise them. In any case I have simplified them sufficiently for a non-judo man to follow them without too much difficulty although they will not be as easy to work out as the counters described in the early part of this book.

CHAPTER XIII

THE SHOULDER THROW

The Shoulder Throw Counter to a right-hand push or punch

Your opponent pushes or strikes at your left shoulder or jaw with his right hand, possibly having

Fig. 67

taken a grip on your jacket. Grip his right sleeve with your left hand below his elbow, having checked his blow as shown in Fig. 1, and pull him in the direction of his push, turning to your left on your right foot as you do so. Keep your body curved slightly forward as you turn, in order to maintain your balance and increase the power of your movement. As you turn bring your right arm through between you and your opponent and place it under and round his right upper

Fig. 68

arm, gripping his arm between the crook of your upper arm and forearm at the elbow. There is no need to grip his jacket with your right hand, although it might help (Fig. 67). As you turn keep on pulling his right arm forward and upward so that when your back is turned directly towards your opponent he is held closely against you, and when your turn is completed, continue the pull and drive your hips back into him. If as you push your hips back you continue your turn to the left and your pull forward with your arm, your attacker will be dumped over your shoulder to the ground very like a sack of coal (Fig. 68). Incidentally

in the initial movement as you begin your turn you may
have to move your feet a little to make the movement
reasonably easy. For example as you have checked his
arm with your left hand it maybe better, as you com-

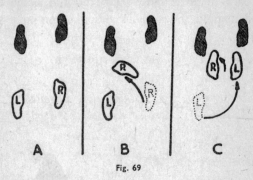

Fig. 69

mence your turn, to step in with your right foot so that
the toes are near the toes of his right foot (Fig. 69).
Don't worry if this is necessary, just do it if it makes
the counter easier.

Shoulder Throw Counter to a Downward Blow

Your opponent attempts to strike at your head
or neck with a stick or knife, raising his weapon and
bringing it directly downwards. Check his blow
with your left forearm, checking his forearm not
the weapon, as described on page 18, and Fig. 1.
Now with your left arm keep his arm up and guide
it to your left, and as soon as possible grip his
sleeve with your left hand. Turn just as described
for the counter to the push on page 120 and bring off

your Shoulder Throw. This is made very much more easy if the attacker persists in trying to force his weapon downwards. If however he should attempt to withdraw his arm for a second blow and perhaps step back to break clear follow up and as he raises his arm apply the armlock described on page 19.

Shoulder Throw and a Counter to a Strangle Hold from the Front

To strangle effectively from the front against a person standing up it is necessary to push forward to obtain sufficient pressure and as a result the attacker leaves himself open for the Shoulder Throw and other counters. Let us assume that the attacker makes the usual form of attack with his right hand at the left side of your neck, thumb digging into your throat, and the left hand taking a similar hold on your right side. Move back to relax the pressure and grasp his right sleeve with both your hands pulling his arm upward and forward—to his front

Fig. 70

—as you do so. At the same time turn your body to your left, curving it forward, by stepping in with your right foot so that your toes are close to the toes of his right foot, and then turning on the ball of your right foot (Fig. 69). Continue the turn and upward and forward pull on your opponent's right sleeve until you have your back towards him. Go on turning until your back makes contact with the front of his body, then drive your hips back into him. The drive with your hips, pull on his right sleeve and turn of your body to the left will force him into a fall over your right shoulder (Fig. 70).

Note.

It greatly helps when performing shoulder and hip throws if, as you commence the counter, you lower your body by bending your knees. This brings your centre of gravity—say your hips, below those of your opponent.

CHAPTER XIV

THE HIP THROW

I am using this description very loosely as I propose to describe as hip throws all throws of this general type not included in the "Shoulder" group just described. Generally it is safe to say that all blows or pushes aimed at your chest and above can be countered with Shoulder Throws whilst the answer to all blows aimed at lower parts of the body can be dealt with by throws of the "Hip" group. This is not to say that other forms of counter such as the Body Drop (see page 136) will not answer just as well, but I want to make the limitations of Hip and Shoulder throws quite clear. I propose to include as Hip Throws all those types of throw in which you place the arm round the opponents waist, shoulders or neck, providing the hips act as the fulcrum or pivot for the throw. This comment is made for the benefit of judo men who will know just what I mean and understand how much more simple this is for beginners.

Hip Throw Counter to a Blow to the Stomach

A punch is aimed at your stomach by your opponent

who uses his right hand. Check and deflect the blow with your left forearm guiding your attacker's arm past your left side. Keeping the outward (to your left) pressure against the attacking arm step in towards him with your left foot, placing it down so that the toes are as close as possible to the toes of his left foot

Fig. 71

(Fig. 71) and turn to your right on your left foot, swinging your left hip in towards him, and taking your right leg back in a circle away from him. Whilst doing this, bring your left arm round his waist. As your left hip makes contact with his body lift him into it with your left arm with a firm inward and at the same time upward pressure, and by continuing the right turn throw him to the ground (Fig. 72). At the earliest possible opportunity during the throw grab his left sleeve or left side of his jacket with your right hand and pull him round you to your right with it as you turn.

An alternative way of dealing with this form of attack is to check his blow with your left forearm as before, again stepping in with your left foot, but this time move it to the vicinity of the toes of his right foot. As you do this grip his right sleeve with your left hand and pull his arm hard in the direction of his original blow, and turning to your left on your left foot, make contact with his body with your right hip. During your turn to your left bring your right arm round his waist or neck and pull him close to you so that he is

Fig. 72

drawn on to your right hip, and then thrown to the ground as your turn is continued.

In both these left- and right-handed Hip Throws what you do in effect is to balance your opponent on your hips and then, by continuing your turn, move away from beneath him which makes him, now unsupported, fall to the ground.

Judo enthusiasts will I'm sure note that I advocate advancing the left foot in both my Hip Throw counters to left and right. I do this, not because it is the best or most effective judo, but because to step in with the left foot whilst checking with the left arm is the more natural movement and as such must be more effective for self-defence, which relies on instinctive reaction.

Note.

It is not absolutely necessary for self-defence purposes to make your turn on the foot mentioned in my description of the hip throws as you are not likely to suffer a judo type counter throw. If it is more convenient or easier, turn on the other foot.

CHAPTER XV

THE STOMACH THROW

This, one of the most famous of all judo throws, is most effective against an opponent who pushes directly forward against you. It does not matter whether or not he crouches in his attack, as long as he leans forward throwing his balance in this direction. This throw follows directly the judo principle. "Move your body out of the line of attack and leave a foot or something for him to fall over." This is such an excellent and effective self-defence throw that I'm sure I will be forgiven if I devote considerable space to it.

The Stomach Throw Counter to an Attack when you are Standing

Imagine, then, that the attacker grips your jacket with both hands and tries to force you down, and back, possibly intending to butt your face with the top of his head. He could of course, equally well be attempting to strangle you. Do not attempt to push back, but grip his sleeves or jacket in your turn and pull him upward and forward, at the same time sitting down on your own left heel, or as near to it as possible. As you sit down his push will be

Fig. 73

directed immediately over you and he will tend automatically to fall forward over you. (Fig. 73). Now roll back, keeping your head well tucked in, and place your right foot into his stomach, pushing him up and over towards your head (Fig. 74) as you roll. Do not thrust him directly upwards, but just use your leg as a lever or fulcrum and then when his body has passed the upright or half-way position push him back to your rear over your head. Be careful at this stage for if you are careless or are in a panic you can catch a very nasty crack in the face from the top of his head. All you have to do to avoid this is to move your head a little to the right or left

Fig. 74

as required to keep clear. Generally speaking it is safe to say that you should move your head to your left if you use your right foot for the throw, and to the right if you use your left foot. Continue your roll to throw him well clear of you, letting go your grip on his jacket with your hands. If you are an athletic type it is not impossible to continue your roll so that you do a gymnastic backward roll, finishing up on your feet near your opponent so that you can put in a finishing kick or blow. If you hold on to his jacket instead of letting go you can even finish up astride him in a wonderful position for using the knee or fist to his body, but although I've seen this described in judo books I'm certain that this successfully carried out is the result of pure luck and not skill or practice. Despite this, however, this roll continued as I have described will bring you into a position of great advantage, even if not that of perfection. If you do not roll right over—and very few people can or will—I most certainly don't— you must get up immediately in order to continue the battle before your opponent recovers or, if discretion is the better part of valour, and often it is, to get well clear before the attacker recovers and gets to his feet.

Alternative Form of Stomach Throw

Some readers may find this variation of the throw more easy to perform, although I consider the usual type of throw not only more effective, but easier to perform with success—and by success I mean putting your attacker out of the fight. In this variation the

opponent once more pushes you straight backwards
or uses a similar form of attack, and you commence
this throw in exactly the same way as the other. That
is by pulling him directly to his front and slightly
upwards, and sitting down close to your left heel
as you do so. This of course has the effect of making
him push against nothing, and the natural tendency
is for him to stumble forward. As he does so use
your foot as a fulcrum over which you allow him to
lever himself, making certain of success by still pulling
with your arms all the time. In this variation, although
you want him to go straight over you in a full Stomach
Throw he is either too heavy or too strong for you,
so success is at least unlikely. This time as he balances
on your foot make no further effort to take him
directly over, but thrust with your foot and throw
him to your left or right side making sure he falls
clear of you on his back or side by pushing with your
arms. If you are throwing him with your right foot
you will normally find it easier to throw him to your
left and if using your left foot to your right. Take
instant advantage of his fall which will undoubtedly
shake him, the best method being to turn over to
face him, driving your knee or elbow, or both, into
his body.

The Stomach Throw Counter to an Attack when you are on the Ground

This time let us assume you have fallen or been

struck to the ground, but have had the opportunity to turn on to your back and use your legs to defend yourself. This method of defence is described on page 65 but your attacker might attempt to bull-doze his way past your legs and bend over you or more likely he'll try and strangle you from above or punch at your face. Immediately grab his jacket at the shoulders or even better as it controls his arms, grasp his sleeve at the level of his elbows if you can possibly do so. Where you hold him does not really matter as long as you make your throw success-fully. Now push him with your arms upwards and to your rear—that is in the direction of your head—and bring your foot, whichever one is more con-venient, up into his stomach, carrying on with the normal Stomach Throw (Fig. 74). You continue with your push and use your leg to wheel him up and over your head, or if this is difficult, dump him on the ground on to his side.

If there is not room between you and your oppo-nent to bring your foot up into his stomach, use your shin and instep instead. If you use your right leg throw him off to your right side when his feet begin to lift above the level of his head.

Note.

When attempting a stomach throw it is essential that you keep rolling back. It is roll which throws your opponent over you. Unless you are very strong do not attempt to make the throw by using your foot against his body only.

Defence on the Ground against an opponent astride you

It is essential to rid yourself of the usual feeling of helplessness when in this admittedly unfortunate position. Although weak, this position on the ground with your opponent sitting astride your body is by no means helpless, but action has to be taken fast. Later I will describe an armlock from this underneath position and now I will explain how it is pos-

Fig. 75

sible to roll your opponent off you and probably reverse the position. Assume that your attacker has gained this position of supposed advantage on top of you and has grabbed your clothing or throat with his right hand. Immediately hold his right wrist with your left hand or better still hold the end of his sleeve (Fig. 75). At the same time grip his clothing at his right shoulder with your right hand and by driving to your right with your left hand and to your left with your right you will tend to upset his balance to his right (Fig. 75). That is he will tend to fall to your left side. If as you do this you lift your right hip violently and withdraw your left hip underneath you to your left your opponent will be thrown off you hard.

You can put the matter beyond doubt by bringing up your right elbow and crashing it against his jaw as you push with your right hand. You will notice that the grip with your right hand brings your right arm between your face and your opponent which helps to protect you from his blows.

CHAPTER XVI

THE BODY DROP (TAIOTOSHI)

One of judo's most popular throws the Body Drop is of even greater use in self-defence, as to make it succeed against an opponent who is holding or pushing you and knows nothing of judo requires very little manoeuvring and usually the attacker throws himself. I was tempted to say that this throw does not require much skill from the self-defence point of view, but I am not quite sure that this is correct, although I feel that a little practice will make it a most effective weapon in the hands of the average person. Its great advantages are that it is not necessary to obtain close contact with your opponent, also it works efficiently against a much stronger and heavier person. To perform it successfully against a person who practises judo naturally requires great skill.

The Body Drop as a Counter to a Hold or Strangle from the front

Your opponent attempts to strangle you from the front with straight arms, his thumbs digging into your throat. Immediately bring your left arm over his right and clasp your hands together, your right arm remaining below his left (Fig. 76). Turn into your Body Drop Throw by taking your left foot back and to your right, passing it behind your right foot (Fig. 77b), as you do so pressing up with your

Fig. 76

right arm and down with your left. As soon as you have placed your left foot on the ground transfer your balance to it and stretch your right foot out so that it is against the front of your attacker's right foot (Figs. 76 and 77c). If you continue your turn

to your left on your left foot and maintain the pressure
of your arms you will find your opponent hurled over
your right leg to the ground.

In the early stages it is essential to move straight
into the counter as soon as the attack is made. To

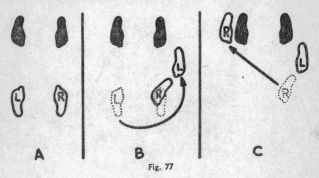

Fig. 77

panic and struggle furiously to take his hands away
from your throat is futile, and means that it will then
be too late to attempt effective counter measures.

Another form of attack against which the Body
Drop is effective is a grip on your clothing or hair.
If the grip is taken with the right hand the throw
is made right-handed—that is similar to that shown
on Fig. 13 on page 35—but a grip with the left hand
calls for a left-handed throw as a counter and all
the moves described and illustrated must be reversed,
that is you turn to your right, moving your right
foot first. Assuming that the grasp on you is made
with the right hand you should grip your opponent's
sleeve with your left hand below his elbow, or as

near to that as you are able to get. Your right hand should find a hold on his jacket on his left lapel or the front of his left shoulder (Fig. 78). Now turn as I have described for the Body Drop counter to the strangle and make the throw in the same way.

Fig. 78

It is quite likely that as your attacker realises his danger he will relax the hold on your body or clothing with his arms and this will make your throw more difficult to carry out, maybe impossible. In this one pull him close to you as soon as you feel him relax and use the Shoulder Throw (page 120), the Hip Throw described on page 125 or the Major Outer Reaping described on page 143.

The Body Drop Throw as a Counter to Attacks from the Rear

I have already described this form of counter in a rather crude way on pages 21, but I would like to mention one or two points for the student of judo or more advanced self-defence man such as commando trained people. Fig. 36 on page 63 shows the hold round the body and arms from behind. Loosen the hold as described by thrusting outwards with your elbows and bending your knees to lower your body and grip your attacker's right sleeve with both hands as high up his arm as possible. Now step forward and a little to your left with your left foot, pulling your opponent forward as you do so. As soon as you have placed your weight and balance on your left foot stretch back your right leg so that it is outside and pressing against your opponent's right foot (Fig. 76), and proceed with the throw by turning to your left. You must make contact against the lower part of his leg with the "hook" at the back of your heel.

The Dropping Version of the Body Drop Throw (Taiotoshi)

This version is used against an opponent who is too strong or heavy for you and manages to resist your Body Drop attempt by pulling back, pushing forward with his arms. Continue your attempt to turn and in addition to pulling him forward with your arms lift him a little in order to bring his balance as much forward as possible. Still continuing these movements lean even further forward and drop on your left knee. The fact that your body suddenly vanishes will make him lose

his balance completely and your throw, now a very
vicious one, is almost certain to succeed. Fig. 79 is

Fig. 79

Fig. 80

drawn from a photograph of the throw being performed in judo practice by two of Canada's leading judo enthusiasts.

The Body Drop as a Counter to a stick attack

You are attacked by an opponent who strikes down at your head with his right hand. Check his arm

Fig. 81

with your left forearm, stepping in with your left foot (Fig. 80) and immediately grip his right sleeve with your right hand. Now keep him coming forward by pulling his right arm to his front and drive your left elbow down on his. At the same time push out your left leg so that it is against his left leg (Fig. 81). A brisk turn to your right will throw him over your left leg to the ground. This is, of course, a left-handed throw. In figure 81 the defender (white jacket) has placed his leg a little too far up his opponent's leg for maximum effect.

CHAPTER XVII

THE MAJOR OUTER REAPING THROW
(O-SOTO-GARI)

This powerful throw is one of the most useful in self-defence. It is a rear throw, that is your opponent is thrown to his rear, and it combines very easily with blows to your opponent's body. In a close quarter attack it is more likely than most other forms of counter attack to conclude the struggle in your favour without further ado. In addition it does not require so much skill as the throws in which you have to turn to make them successful and for this reason it is much safer to attempt. That is to say it does not suffer from leaving you in a difficult position should the attempt fail.

The Major Outer Reaping Throw as a Counter to an Attack from the Front

Let us assume that your opponent attacks from your front with an attempt to strangle you. Alternatively he might grab your clothing with his left hand whilst he strikes with his right at your face or chest. In either case immediately turn your body sideways to him and check the initial blow or break up his strangle as described in the earlier chapters.

The turn not only protects your body from attempts to kick or strike with the knee but also brings you closer to him for your own counter-attack. If he holds you with his left hand only, bring in your left shoulder, presenting the left side of your body to him, or if his hold is right-handed bring in your right shoulder. If you try this you will find the reason quite obvious. In this way you do not try and advance against the strength of the arm holding you. A hold with both arms demands a different technique. You must lower your body by bending your knees in order to attack upwards, so again avoiding the attacker's full strength. Whether you advance with your left or right shoulder in this case depends on personal preference, but it is certain that the best way is the way which appears stronger to you, but should he appear weaker on one side than the other always attack that weaker side. If, of course, he lets go with either arm immediately advance the side which has just been released.

Assume then that the attacker is right-handed and grips your clothing with his left hand whilst he strikes with his right. Check his right arm as already described with your left forearm and keeping your arm inside his, continue your forward movement to grip his clothing in the area of his right shoulder. Where does not matter, you can place your arm round his neck or waist if that is the natural movement, but take care to release it as he falls. The vicinity of his left hip as shown in Fig. 82 is a good place for the grip. As you take your grip on his clothing with your left hand continue to turn to your right, driving your left shoulder into his chest—you should have turned in the initial check of his blow—and hook your left leg behind his left (Fig. 82) gripping his left sleeve with

Fig. 82

your right hand. At this stage drive down with your left arm and in towards you with your right, and push your left shoulder against his chest. At the same time pull his left leg towards you with your own hooked left leg. All this is shown in Fig. 82. This resulting throw hurls him on to his back and he will take a very severe shock.

Should this form of attack be reversed, your opponent holding you with his right hand and punching with his left, the defence and throw are exactly the same, except that the initial defence against the punch is carried out with your right hand and the turn is made to your left. Every movement being carried out exactly opposite to the left hand counter I have just described. If, on practice, you find it easier to turn to your left after checking a right-hand blow with your left forearm, of course do so.

A Variation to the Major Outer Reaping Defence

Judo-wise readers will have realised that I have described the throw left-handed. This is more difficult than the right-handed version and one of the reasons that pupils at a judo club should learn their throws on both sides. I ·have had to use the left-handed throw for a counter to a right-hand attack as this is the natural movement—the continuation of the original check. However, although not quite such a natural movement the easier right-handed throw can be used instead.

Again you are faced with an opponent who is holding you with his left hand and attempting to strike with his right. Again check his blow outwards with your left arm and immediately you have done this grip his right sleeve with your left hand, somewhere by the elbow if possible. As you check his blow, of course you have stepped in with your left foot turning your left side towards the attacker Now bring your right leg and side through, using your right knee to deal a blow to his body as you do so, and hook the back of his right leg with your right leg. Grip his coat with your right hand near his left shoulder and press down on him with both hands, hooking his leg as you do so and driving your right shoulder forward into him. As a result he will be hurled straight over your right leg to the ground, landing on his back or more likely his head or shoulders. The throw technique is exactly the same as for the left-handed throw and although reversed the position is shown quite clearly in Fig. 82 on page 145.

The Inside Leg Throw (O-Uchi-Gari)

Another vigorous and effective throw is the Inside Leg Throw. From the judo point of view it requires more skill to make it as effective as the Major Outer Reaping, but from the self-defence aspect it is equally effective and in some respects not so difficult to apply. It is not anticipated that it will have to be used in self-defence against an experienced judo man. This throw, like the Major Outer Reaping, requires you to check the right-hand blow or punch with your left arm, advancing your left leg, as you do so in order to present that side of your body to your opponent. This time you continue to advance the left leg, hooking the inside of your attacker's right leg and grabbing his jacket with both hands somewhere near the shoulders. As you hook his leg backwards—to your rear—pull him down with your arms and drive your left shoulder into his chest. Again he will be thrown heavily over your left leg to the ground.

Here, once more, I have described the natural defence which is the more difficult left-hand throw. You can use the right-hand throw instead in exactly the way I described on page 146 for the Major Outer Reaping, carrying out all the movements I have just taught, but on the other side.

CHAPTER XVIII

THE DRAWING ANKLE THROW
(TSURI-KOMI-ASHI)

One of the most popular throws, the Drawing Ankle is not easy and should only be attempted in self-defence by a person sufficiently experienced to see the proper opening or opportunity. Fortunately a failure will not have you in a weak position, but it does give the attacker another opportunity to attack. Successfully performed, it is one of the neatest and most effortless throws possible to imagine and I should think the sensation of floating into the air and then falling hard as the result of no apparent effort would discourage most attackers. It is throws of this type which give judo its unearned reputation as a mysterious and secret rite which is performed at a flick of the fingers by a selected few. Actually, of course, success only comes as a result of hard work and a throw of this description requires a combination of good timing, balance and speed.

The Drawing Ankle Throw as a Counter to a Blow

This time your opponent aims a blow with his right arm at your head or chest.

The target does not matter provided the blow is aimed fairly high. If we imagine that you are attacked and your opponent strikes at your jaw with his right fist, you first ward off his blow to your left with your left forearm. In this case you deflect his arm upwards and to your left. As the deflection is made, catch his right jacket sleeve with your left hand at any convenient point and pull him with that hand in the direction of his blow. This will bring him up on his toes off balance.

Continue your pull and grip his jacket somewhere with your right hand and push in the same direction

Fig. 83

as that in which your left hand is pulling in order to make him step forward with his left foot, or at least throw his balance over it. As he does so bring the sole of your left foot up against his right shin and continue your pull. You should find your opponent thrown over your left foot to the ground. In fact he appears to throw himself (Fig. 83).

Should the blow be aimed lower at your stomach, check it downwards and outwards with your left arm, and again obtain a grip on his jacket sleeve as soon as possible. You pull in the direction of his blow, which in this case is downwards, and to your left, and since his body as a result of the nature of the blow and your defence is lower and probably bent forward, you will have to lower your own body to make your throw successful. In order to do this all that is necessary is to bend your right knee and curve your body forward. This throw is far more difficult as the attacker is bent forward.

The Rolling Ankle Throw

This is exactly the same in principle as the Ankle

Fig. 84

Throws just described, but is more effective against a heavy or powerful attacker. In this case you check the

blow in exactly the same way, but as you make contact
with the sole of the foot against his shin you allow
yourself to fall as you turn to your left (Fig. 84).
In other words you make as large or wide a circle
as you possibly can with your body pivoting on your
right foot, finishing up on the ground on your left side
as shown in Fig. 85. The advantages of this version
of the throw are the far greater leverage obtained
on your opponent, and the attack being made much
lower and well below his centre of gravity. In addition

Fig. 85

your opponent is thrown not only with the weight
of his body but also with all the power and momentum
of your own movement, which has all the weight of
your own body behind it.

It is only fair to point out the disadvantages. The
throw requires a practical knowledge of judo technique and should not be attempted by the casual
reader, or even the thorough reader who has not
practised judo as a sport. It is essential to make the

throw by continually withdrawing the left hip so that the left hip is the first part of your body to touch the ground—this is difficult. Finally, and probably most important, you are in a very weak position on the ground if your throw fails as it might if mistimed or attempted when the opportunity does not exist. It is advisable to take up the defensive position shown in Fig. 38 on page 66, automatically as the throw, or attempt, is completed without waiting to see the result. My advice is do not attempt this throw unless you have been taught it personally by a competent instructor.

The Ankle Throw to the Rear (Ko-Soto-Gari)

I am sure I shall be told that the use of this throw is unnecessary in self-defence as if the opportunity arises to use it the Major Outer Reaping would be found equally effective, and is far more simple for the novice or person unpractised in judo to perform. This may well be true but the Rear Ankle Throw is so simple in theory and so neat and graceful if successful that I feel justified in including it. In addition this part of the book is intended to back up the basic judo throws with self-defence for the enthusiast.

The Rear Ankle Throw as a Counter to a pull or hold on the Hair or Clothing

The Throw can be brought off on most occasions

when the attacker does not push or lean forward. His body must be upright with his balance at least central over his feet, and if possible he should be pulling you forward to his rear. If his knees are bent as he pulls all the better.

The attacker grips you somehow with one or both hands at chest level or above and attempts to drag you forward. You must take the usual preliminary precaution of advancing your left foot to bring the side of your body towards him in order to minimise

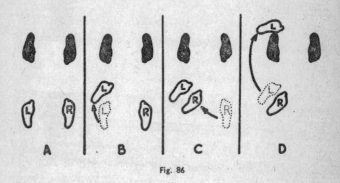

Fig. 86

the result of a possible kick or blow with his knee (Fig. 86b) and grab your opponent's jacket anywhere in your turn and pull him towards you. This not only brings you into closer contact but will, quite possibly, goad him into pulling even harder. As his pull continues bring your right foot up close to your left (Fig. 86c) and still hold him as close to you as possible. Follow up by bringing the sole of your left foot behind his right ankle (Fig. 86d), and pull

Fig. 87

forward towards your opponent's toes with it. If you can get your left foot far enough round to trap his left ankle all the better. As you trap his ankle reverse your pull and turn it into a downward and backward push so that he is thrown back over your left foot (Fig. 87). His own pull will make him throw himself whilst your sudden change from a pull to a push will make the throw unexpected and violent.

An Alternative (Ko-Uchi-Gari)

It is quite possible to trap the back of the attacker's left ankle from the inside with your left foot instead of the back of his right ankle with your left foot. This works on the same principle and has the advantage that it can be effected without any of the appreciable movement of your feet required in the Throw shown in Fig. 86, or at least you only have to move it a very little. In practice, however, the Inside Ankle Throw, that is what this is called, is much more difficult to bring off successfully and I cannot advise the novice at judo to attempt it. It is, however, a useful throw for the more experienced reader to bear in mind.

In this throw the blow, which is right handed is checked with the left arm and the left leg advanced as usual. As soon as possible—that is a continuation of the initial check of the blow—you grip his jacket with both hands and trap the back of his left ankle with the sole of your left foot from the inside. Now bear down and push violently to your opponent's left rear with your hands and pull his left leg forward with your left foot.

Because it is natural to advance the right leg as a right-handed punch is made it is essential to attack the right ankle as a counter to a right-handed blow or push Although you take away his right foot you must not push your opponent to his rear, but downwards.

Note.

I have stated in my description of the Rear and Inside Ankle Throws that your throw is made with the sole of your foot. This is the correct judo method, but if you are wearing hard shoes or boots you might find that it gives a better result to hook your opponent's ankle with the top of your foot, using the angle between your foot and shin as a hook.

CHAPTER XIX

USEFUL METHODS OF BREAKING HOLDS ON YOUR BODY AND CLOTHING

Although strictly forbidden in judo when practised as a sport a very useful method of breaking these holds is to attack single fingers and thumbs with the whole power of your arm, or better still, body. This form of counter-attack can be brought into use almost any time, providing you can reach your opponent's hand and, having reached the hand you propose to attack, are in a position to apply leverage against it. For example, it is useless to try to move the opponent's hand if you are so placed that you can only just reach it and having done so are in such an awkward position that you are unable to apply at least the whole power of your arm. Such a position might well be a hold round your body from the front, your attacker clasping his hands together behind you. No doubt you could fairly easily reach behind you and grip his hand, but the grip would be so awkward and uncomfortable that it would be completely useless to you. I will, however, describe some of the occasions when counter-attacking the fingers is likely to be successful.

Note.

You should always attack an opponent's thumb with the hand which is the same side as the thumb to be attacked. This will be made clear as the counters are described. The thumb is usually attacked because it is isolated, the fingers being kept tightly and safely together.

Countering a Grip on the Hair

The attacker grips your hair from the front with his right hand, no doubt intending to pull you forward and to the ground. Instead of countering with the Arm Lock described on page 32 bring up both your hands using your left to hold his wrist or hand close to your head, thus reducing the pull whilst your right grips his thumb. Wrench the thumb— still assuming it to be his right—upwards and to your right, turning to your right as you do so, and you should force him to release his hold at once. As soon as you have done so continue with a counter-attack such as a blow to his body with your left knee and a throw to your left such as the Major Outer Reaping, described on page 143, using your left leg to hook his left leg.

Countering a Grip on the Clothing

Here the position is much the same except that the hold is more likely to be made with the left hand, so leaving the right free for some other form of attack. Here again you should attack the thumb of the hand with which he is holding, in this case his left, but this time with your left, or if possible both hands. Place both your hands on his, gripping his thumb and turn sharply to your left. The pain of his thumb being forced away from his fingers should force him to release his hold. As he does so your counter should follow up hard and fast.

Countering a Strangle Hold from the Front

It is safe to assume that the attack will be made in the usual thug style. His left hand will be on the right side of your neck, and his right hand on the left with the thumbs of both hands digging into your throat in the middle. Naturally move back to try and ease the hold and give yourself a little time to counter and clasp whichever of his thumbs is uppermost with both hands, moving it sharply upwards and away from you. You might be able to hold a thumb in each hand and take the same action, but this is unlikely, although quite possible. Anyway you must force the thumb away from the fingers and in the opposite direction to that in which the hand naturally closes—away from the palm.

Wrist Locks

These locks require a certain amount of physical strength. It is not necessary to be strong or nearly as strong as your opponent but the lock has to be applied firmly and quickly, and I very much doubt whether a girl could bring it off against even a reason-ably weak man. For this reason it is important to apply the whole of your weight and power when the lock is attempted. The lock itself is another of those which can be used against holds on the hair or clothing, anywhere down to chest level. As an example I pro-pose to take a right-handed grip on your clothing at chest level.

As soon as the hold is taken, place the palms of both your hands, one on top of the other, on the

Fig. 88

back of your attacker's hand, pressing it as hard as you can against your own body, and not allowing him to release his hold. Now keeping on the pressure curve your body forward and step sharply back, at the same time bending forward. This will have the effect of forcing his wrist down and back and will at least force the hold to be released, and no doubt cause painful injury to his wrist. (Fig. 88).

If you are strong in the wrists it is possible to grip his hand with your thumbs on the palm of his hand and fingers on the back of it, and by just pushing towards him with the thumbs and pressing your fingers down and towards you, you obtain the same effect. Of course a combination of both movements is ideal.

Leg Locks

These locks are forbidden in judo because the knee is particularly liable to injury. In addition, these injuries are painful and take a long time to heal. Self-defence is, however, a different matter altogether, for the attacker deserves all he receives as a result of any self-defence technique that may be used against him.

For the purpose of your practice it is as well to remember that the danger of injury arises not so much from the application of the lock but from your opponent's efforts to escape the lock once you have commenced to apply it. As long as the leg is kept straight or at least bent in the line of the leg there is no danger of anything worse than a certain amount of pain, but as soon as your opponent attempts to turn his body over, possibly from lying on his back to his side, or from face down to his back, the danger of a serious knee injury is considerable, providing you maintain your hold. This should be remembered for the purpose of practice but in serious self-defence the lock should be held strongly and your opponent allowed to take the consequences of his struggles.

The Standing Leg Lock

This lock might be applied as a counter to a kick, this is certainly the most obvious chance of using it. Your opponent attempts to kick you, aiming at

Fig. 89

the stomach with the toe of his right boot and you counter by checking his attack with a downward and outward chop of your right forearm and at the same time turning your body away from him by advancing your left foot and so presenting your left hip to him. This is described on page 46. As soon as you have deflected his leg past you slide your right arm—the one used for the defence—over or under his leg as convenient, pinning it between your arm and body. At the same time step sharply back in order to pull him off his left foot and so throw him on to his back. Now retain your hold on his leg and lock it with the ankle under your armpit, his actual foot behind your shoulder (Fig. 89), and the sharp, thumb side, of your forearm across the back of his leg, as low down his leg as possible. Try to get it somewhere near the Achilles tendon. Apply the lock by pulling hard upwards against his leg with your forearm, clasping your hands and using the strength of both arms if you like.

The Leg Lock on the Ground

This is exactly the same lock in application, his leg being held under your armpit with his foot and just behind your shoulder. The lock is effected by the upward pull of the sharp bony edge of your forearm, that is the thumb side, against his leg as low down towards his foot as possible. This lock can be used should you attempt the standing lock and lose your balance, or more likely the opportunity will arise in a scramble on the ground. The main difference in this version of the lock is that your opponent can release the pressure on his leg by bending his knee. He cannot, of course, do this to the standing version as the weight of his body and your upward and backward pull prevent it. To avoid this you must use your leg or legs, whichever is the more convenient and comfortable to pin him down by using them to press down on his body.

Actually it is only necessary to pin him just above his knees, there is no need to go any higher up his body, although this is usually more comfortable and gives a greater feeling of confidence. Should you do so you will find it easier to control your opponent, but you always stand the chance of the attacker also knowing the lock and attempting to apply it on you in return. The ideal position is shown in Fig. 90.

Should you be knocked or pushed to the ground and find your opponent standing over you you may

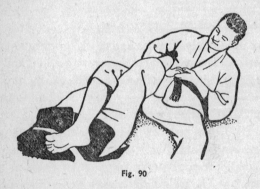

Fig. 90

find the opportunity to attempt the lock. To do this you must be able to catch one of his ankles, if possible getting your arm round it at your elbow. Pull his leg towards you and using the most convenient leg push or kick your opponent over backwards, pulling his leg towards you into the leg lock position (Figs. 89 and 90) as he falls, and pinning his body down with your legs immediately he strikes the ground, adopting the position shown in Fig. 90.

When using these locks it does not really matter which of his legs you attack or under which arm you pull his foot. Nor does it matter with which leg you pin him to the ground, or even if you use both legs perhaps crossing them over his body.

The Bent Leg Lock

Here we have another form of Leg Lock which is just as easy to apply and equally effective. Similarly it can be applied from a standing position or during a struggle on the ground. As it is easy to see the opening whilst fighting on the ground if the method is fully understood, I do not propose to describe the lock separately for each form, but will concentrate on it from the standing position. The best opening occurs when your opponent attacks by kicking at your body. As usual ward off the blow with your forearm and catch his leg with your arm as soon as possible, probably by pinning it between your arm and body. This time your opponent turns his body as he kicks, he might have attempted the judo type kick described on page 22, so that when your pull on his leg takes effect he falls to the ground face downwards. Assuming that you warded off and caught his leg with your right arm, drive forward so that you make him bend his leg at the knee and place your right leg across the back of his knee

Fig. (91). Using your leg as a fulcrum continue to force his leg up so that the angle of his calf and back of his thigh close on your leg like a V. Continue to drive forward forcing his leg to close up on the

Fig. 91

leg you are using as a wedge. Pushing on his foot with your shoulder will add to your leverage. This form of lock causes intense pain, and if applied fast and with a jerk could easily dislocate and cause permanent damage to your opponent's knee. You can accept my word that a dislocation is unbelievably painful so take it very slowly when practising with a friend.

CHAPTER XX

THE USE OF BLOWS IN SELF-DEFENCE (ATEMI)

Normally in judo clubs the use of atemi, that is the violent and deadly blows dealt with your elbows, fingertips, knees and so on to your opponent's nerve centres are not taught until Black Belt grade is reached. This is mainly in order that the wrong type of person does not receive tuition, but so many judo and self-defence books contain mentions of this section of defence that I think this book would be incomplete without a chapter on the subject, especially as I have mentioned the use of one such blow, the attack with the knee to the groin, on several occasions. I have compromised to a certain extent, as I have in general only included blows which are basically defensive in that they are used at close quarters. Others, which in my opinion would be of great use to the type of person who would use them for aggressive purposes I have left out.

The Vital Points of the Body

Fig. 92 shows the vital points of the body. Some have been mentioned when I have been describing counters to various attacks, but others have been ignored. It will be quite clear from the diagram

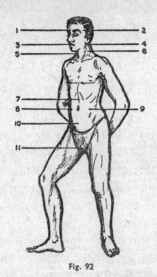

Fig. 92

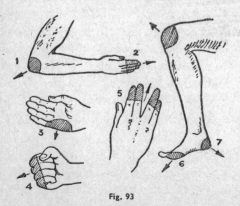

Fig. 93

and also Fig. 93 how these points should be attacked
in self-defence and to assist I shall add a few notes
in each case.

Look at Fig. 92, the marks show some of the more
accessible of the vulnerable points of the body. They
are :—

1. The middle of the forehead. This is best attacked
    with the fist against an upright opponent, with
    the knee, if your opponent crouches or with
    the ball of the foot, heel, knee or fist if you are
    both on the ground.

2. The temples are vulnerable to the same forms
    of attack as the middle of the forehead. These
    are described in paragraph 1 above.

3. The cleft between the upper lip and nose,
    open to attack with the edge of the hand or finger-
    tips. As a general rule the fist is too large to
    attack this point with effect, in any case the fist
    is a very overrated weapon.

4. The back of the neck should be attacked with
    what is known to all schoolboys as the "rabbit
    punch." This can be delivered with the fist
    or the edge of the hand.

5. The throat is difficult to attack with the fist,
    but is vulnerable to the edge of the hand or
    fingertips.

6. The carotid arteries at the side of the neck can be attacked with the fist, edge of the hand or fingertips.

7. The pit of the stomach is a well-known spot, generally called the solar plexus. Like the temples and forehead, it should be attacked with the fingertips, fist, knee, foot or heel as the opportunity arises. The blow should be upward, driving under the rib cage.

8 and 9. The right and left sides. All children know of this nerve centre from the earliest days as a result of being tickled. A severe blow here, however, is crippling. The fingertips, fist or knee form the best weapons of attack.

10. The abdominal region or lower part of the stomach is open to attack with the fist or knee or again on the ground additionally with the foot or heel.

11. The groin is best attacked by an upward blow from the knee or foot.

The Parts of the Body used for Striking

These are shown in Fig. 93.

1. The elbow.
2. The fingertips.
3. The edge of the hands.

4.   The fists.

5.   The fingertips to the eyes.

6.   The ball of the foot.

7.   The heel.

Possibly a few notes on the attacking parts of the body would be helpful. The fists, knees, heels and elbow are obvious, and so is the sole of the foot, especially when you are wearing shoes. As you are most unlikely to have to defend yourself whilst bare-footed I shall cover this by referring you to the illustration which makes the kicking position and part of the foot quite clear. The edge of the hand is only effective if the fingers are kept straight and firmly together. The relaxed hand is, of course, no weapon. The striking part is that part of the little finger side of the hand just below the first joint of that finger. To make this attack effective the hand must be used as a whip being flicked at the target and no further. The old idea of a solid blow with a tennis type "follow through" is not nearly so effective and tends to make you lose your balance which can be disastrous if your counter is not decisive.

The hand must also be kept rigid if the attack with the fingertips is to be made effective. Here the fingers must be kept firmly together the jab being aimed at the target and no further, with the same whip-like movement as the side of the hand blow. A certain amount of accuracy is required with this blow as a powerful jab landing on your opponent's jaw will do far more harm to you than it will to him.

One last means of defence is worth description in this section. It is very simple and consists of no more than a wholehearted slap to the face delivered with the open palm of the hand. Considerable shock is caused by this blow and it is easy to follow up with some other form of attack. I'm told of one case where the slap was delivered and followed up with an arm lock. This enabled the intended victim to take his attacker along to the police station without difficulty.

CHAPTER XXI

ARM LOCKS

These must be applied suddenly and hard if they are to put a possibly stronger opponent out of action. They are severe in effect, but I think as a basic self-defence move the blow downwards against the elbow when the arm is straight already described is more effective in circumstances where it is appropriate. Should the victim of the attack be small or a woman it would almost certainly be impossible to apply a standard arm lock effectively, but after the attacker has been "softened up" with a blow or throw or both, it is a different matter. If a struggle should develop on the ground the standard locks might also prove useful, especially if applied with power and a jerk.

Locks against the Straight Arm

There is only one basic lock which is applied on the ground against the elbow. I'll describe four ways of using it, others can be worked out for yourself.

It is important that the pressure should always be applied against the thumb side of the arm, that is to say, always pull against the thumb. If this is not done the arm will naturally bend at the elbow as you apply the lock.

Straight Arm Lock Sideways

The opportunity to apply this often arises in a struggle on the ground when you are at the side

Fig. 94

of your opponent. Grip his sleeve with one hand above the elbow—say his right sleeve—and pull his arm straight, your other hand should grip his wrist. It is always better to take a hold with one hand on the sleeve than to rely solely on the wrist or arm itself, because your opponent will no doubt be hot and both his wrist and your hand slippery, and as a result you are likely to lose your hold. Keep his arm straight, pulling on it all the time, and swing one leg across his body, preferably your left and use that leg to hold him down, across his neck, preventing him turning towards you (Fig 94). If you can get your right leg across as well, the other side of his arm, all the better. Fall back, changing your grip to his wrist and pulling on his arm, so that his elbow is forced back over your thigh and continuing the pull back towards you and down across your thigh. Lift your hips to add to the pressure. This lock especially if used fast, is very powerful and serious damage to his elbow will easily occur. It does not matter in the least across which leg the arm is forced, it depends mainly on the angle at which you lie to his body. Don't pull his arm down directly between your legs—it can be very painful—it must go across your thigh.

Straight Arm Lock across the Thigh

This lock is used from astride your opponent when he pushes against the upper part of your body or face. Perhaps, he pushes you backwards, so you cannot use the lock just described. Instead, pull his arm, I am assuming he is pushing with his left, straight and in the direction of his push and straighten your right leg, pushing it forward. The pull on his arm is towards you, and past your right side.

Fig. 95

As he pushes continue to pull the arm straight and then downwards so that the upper arm is across your right leg (Fig. 95). His elbow should be on or past your leg to ensure that he cannot save himself by bending his arm. If this lock is applied with a jerk your opponent is almost certain to receive a severely damaged arm, so take it slowly in practice, especially as you are very likely to lose your balance backwards.

The Straight Arm Lock from Underneath

It is not correct to assume, as most people do, that the person underneath in a struggle on the ground is in the position of disadvantage. Certainly this is not so if he is trained, even to a fairly small extent, in judo. If you do meet with misfortune and find yourself involved in a struggle of this nature, you must try not to allow your opponent to get into position astride your body. This can be done if your legs are used intelligently, the method is described on page 65, and often results in your opponent finishing up kneeling between your legs and attempting to punch at your face or body or perhaps attacking your throat with his hands. Obtain a grip on his

Fig. 96

right sleeve or wrist with your left or possibly both hands, pulling it towards your head. At the same time draw up your right leg and with your right foot push or kick away his left thigh (Fig. 96). This results in his body being straightened out and tending to collapse on you. At once turn to your right on your right side and bring your left leg up over his outstretched right arm, which you should be keeping

Fig. 97

straight by pulling it towards your head, and push your leg under his head (Fig. 97). You will find that your left leg drives down on his upper arm and if as you do this you push his arm upwards with your hands a severe lock is applied.

There are several similar locks which are very effective from underneath, but if you have a knowledge of judo these can be thought out for yourself, or at least worked out from experience of judo practice and contests. There are a fairly large number; all, or at least most of them are applied by bringing your leg or knee down or sideways against your opponent's arm. They all involve pulling the opponent's arm straight and keeping it so.

A Lock Against the Bent Arm

Very often it is impossible to apply the locks I have described for use against a straight arm, perhaps because being close to you your opponent does not push with straight arms or because of your lack of skill or his strength he manages to bend his arm when you attempt to attack the straight arm. The lock is not easy if you are unskilled, but given judo experience it is devastating even against a much stronger person. I very much doubt if it could be applied successfully by anyone completely untrained in judo.

The Lock from above your Opponent

It is usually applied from beside your opponent. Perhaps he tries to push you away with his left arm

Fig. 98

when you are at his right side. Immediately grasp his left wrist with your left hand and lie across his body, forcing his left wrist down on to the ground with his arm bent like a letter L at the elbow. The arm should be bent so that his upper arm is above his shoulder, as shown in the illustration. Keeping his wrist on the ground bring your right arm under his left shoulder, and hold your own left wrist with the palm of your right hand down (Fig. 98). By holding his wrist on the ground and lifting his shoulder with your right arm you apply a painful lock.

This lock can be applied in the same way if you are astride your opponent, his left wrist being held with your left hand and your right arm coming under his arm to hold your own left wrist. This time, however, your right arm comes more under his elbow—you cannot avoid this—and the lock is therefore less effective. For this reason every effort should be made to keep your right arm as far under the opponent's shoulder as possible, in order to avoid lifting his elbow from the ground when the lock is applied. In both cases it is the shoulder, not the elbow, which is raised by your right arm, the elbow should be kept down as much as possible.

The Lock from Underneath

This form of the lock is not such an effective method of disabling your opponent, but is mainly of use to throw your attacker off you and perhaps cause an injury sufficiently serious to prevent him continuing his attack. It is just possible, if the lock is applied with a severe jerk, that he will be disabled completely, but you must be prepared to follow up the lock in case it only succeeds in rolling him off you.

If your attacker is astride you, you cannot attempt the straight arm lock described on page 177 because you are unable to use your feet to straighten his body. In addition, your opponent will be so close to you that he is most unlikely to have his arms straight. Thus that type of lock is ruled out completely unless you are much stronger than he is. As no cosh boy would attack any person who had, in his opinion, a chance of defending him, or herself, this form of lock, that is forcing the straight arm lock—can be ignored. The situation is almost certain to be that the attacker, once astride you, will attack your throat

Fig. 99

or grip your jacket or clothing with one hand to maintain his balance whilst he punches at your face with the other. If he uses the former attack you can choose which arm you counter as long as you do so quickly, but if the latter attack is used you have no alternative, you must take the hand and arm which he is holding still for you, that is in this case his left. For the purpose of my description I shall assume he holds somewhere near your shoulder with his left hand, so at once bring your left hand across and grip his left wrist. This also brings your arm across you and protects you from his punches to a great degree. Now bring your right arm behind his upper arm and grip your own left wrist with your right hand (Fig. 99) and with a rapid and somewhat violent jerk detach his hand from your jacket and force his arm downwards towards the ground and to his left rear. That is push him down and to your right. As you do so roll to your right and your opponent should be thrown off you to your right side with a disabled left arm.

CHAPTER XXII

SOME FINAL TIPS ON SELF-DEFENCE

Self-defence is not fun. You are liable to find yourself fighting hard to avoid serious injury and so you must expect to be hurt. The methods of self-defence I have described will not prevent you being hurt but will give you a very good chance of emerging the victor without any severe injury. You will have to accept this and should a blow from your opponent break through it is essential, at least for the time being, to ignore the pain caused and instead of allowing it to make you give up it must be used as a spur to counter-attack and victory.

This may not sound very encouraging but the chances of attack can be very greatly reduced if you remain alert and cautious. When walking, especially alone, at night or in lonely places always be alert. Keep an eye on any person who appears to be following you or who approaches. Keep to the outside of the path or in the middle of a lane. Listen for approaching footsteps and watch shadows, that is to say as you pass a street lamp you will see the shadow of anyone behind you thrown up on the ground in front of you. The same thing happens as the result of lights in houses and the headlamps of passing cars. As soon as you see a shadow in these circumstances immediately glance round and see who it is. Always, of course, avoid patches of deep shadow.

In made-up but quiet streets, I repeat, walk on the outside of the pavement. This obviates the chance of anyone jumping out of a house or garden entrance at you to snatch your handbag or brief-case or worse. For exactly the same reason I suggested walking down the middle of a lane where there are no made-up paths and perhaps no street lamps. If you consider it advisable, you can even cross the road to avoid a person of whom you are suspicious. If he follows, he at least makes his attention fairly obvious. Although I am again repeating myself I must emphasise that the success of an attack depends on surprise and if, therefore, you are sufficiently alert to prevent a surprise your counter-attack is half-way to being successful. The main thing is to see the attack coming, which enables you to shout, scream or just concentrate on dealing with the attacker. Make as much noise as possible as this naturally tends to frighten off law-breakers.

In conclusion, may I say I hope I have not frightened the reader and made her or him believe it is not safe to walk along the streets. This was certainly not my intention but newspaper reports lead one to believe that attacks on innocent persons are increasing. This book therefore aims at convincing everyone who picks it up that attacks on them although no doubt most unlikely are possible and if one is prepared it may not only save serious or at least unpleasant injury but will make these thugs think twice about attacking even the smallest looking girl and later, perhaps, having thought twice, they may decide against making the attack.

SOME NOTES ON JUDO

There is very little more I can tell you about self-defence, unless I list and describe dozens of variations and tricks, either for the complete novice or the experienced judo man—I hesitate to use the word expert as so very few Europeans can really claim to have reached that status. My main hope is that I have aroused the reader's interest, especially that of the non-judo reader, so that the attacks which occur regularly receive the reception they deserve. It has never been my ambition that everyone should learn judo, but I sincerely hope that the day will arrive when everyone will know what judo is and be able to appreciate the difference between a properly organised judo club or qualified teacher, and the people who make a living without those qualifications by trading on the glamour which surrounds the words judo and ju-jitsu. A good judo club is like a large store. At a department store you are invited to come along and look round without being pestered to buy. In a similar way the judo club should make you welcome and invite you to watch. Its members should be pleased to answer your questions and advise you, but will not worry you to join. That is left to you. A club which does not welcome visitors and allow them to watch freely is always suspect.

We like you to take up judo as a sport, but only if you are keen to do so—we do not want people to be attracted by the glamour or to believe they will be invincible in six easy lessons.

The big clubs, like my own London Judo Society, run organised beginners' classes, where novices all start together, and work under supervision. The courses are fairly short, say 16 lessons spread over two months, but are designed to give you a very good idea what judo is like as a sport, and leave you reasonably proficient. After that you are invited to join the main club. You will see, therefore, that you can "try out" judo at a small cost and if you find it is not your idea of a sport you can drop out with no obligation or ill-feeling and little cost.

We always welcome beginners at London Judo Society, which is situated at 32, St. Oswald's Place, S.E.11, off Kennington Lane, behind the famous Oval cricket ground. Visitors are welcome between 7 and 9 p.m. every Monday, Tuesday, Wednesday and Friday evening. There are also Junior and Ladies sections. If you do not live in London I will be pleased to try and locate your nearest club for you.

Finally, what does judo do for you? As I have said before, the court reports of most attacks reveal that the attacker was seen or spoken to before the assault, and there is no doubt that judo practised as a sport leaves you more alert and prepared. You learn to react faster, the more practice at judo you have the nearer you are to the time when it becomes instinctive to react to sudden and unexpected movement. No short course or any amount of reading can give you this reaction—only judo practised as a sport for a fairly considerable time. One of the mottos of London Judo Society is:

"Learn judo as a sport and self-defence becomes second nature."

This is very true and all I can say in conclusion is, why not have a try, or at least a look?

INDEX